When Ways of Life *Collide*

MULTICULTURALISM AND
ITS DISCONTENTS IN THE NETHERLANDS

When Ways of Life
Collide

Paul M. Sniderman and
Louk Hagendoorn

PRINCETON UNIVERSITY PRESS

PRINCETON AND OXFORD

Copyright © 2007 by Princeton University Press

Published by Princeton University Press, 41 William Street, Princeton, New Jersey 08540

In the United Kingdom:
Princeton University Press, 3 Market Place, Woodstock, Oxfordshire OX20 1SY

All Rights Reserved

Library of Congress Cataloging-in-Publication Data

Sniderman, Paul M.

When ways of life collide : multiculturalism and its discontents in the
Netherlands / Paul M. Sniderman and Louk Hagendoorn.

p. cm.

Includes bibliographical references and index.

ISBN-13: 978-0-691-12906-8 (hardcover : alk. paper)

ISBN-10: 0-691-12906-1 (hardcover : alk. paper)

1. Muslims—Netherlands. 2. Netherlands—Ethnic relations. 3. Minorities—Netherlands.
4. Multiculturalism—Netherlands. 5. Multiculturalism. I. Hagendoorn, A., 1945– II. Title.

DJ92.M86S64 2007

305.6′9709492—dc22

2006018679

British Library Cataloging-in-Publication Data is available

This book has been composed in Fournier.

Printed on acid-free paper. ∞

pup.princeton.edu

Printed in the United States of America

1 3 5 7 9 10 8 6 4 2

To Anne and Alena
for their affection and companionship

and to Dr. Allan Sniderman,
whose life, discoveries, and family
honor our parents.

CONTENTS

FIGURES

TABLES

OUR CONCERN is the collision between Western European values and Muslim values. Our focus is the Netherlands because it has undertaken the most ambitious policy of multiculturalism. The premise of multiculturalism as a principle is respect for the pluralism of cultures. Yet its thrust as a public policy has been to legitimize and subsidize one particular expression of Muslim culture—ironically the one most at odds with the pluralistic spirit of liberal democracy. Our findings are thus not about multiculturalism in the abstract. They are about what actually happens when issues of group identity are made a focal point of public attention and political argument in the inevitably rough and ready tumble of real politics. We believe, but are not in a position to prove, that our results travel to other countries.

The most important advantage we had in doing this study was doing it too soon. There is a sequence to social science research: a dramatic event happens—say, September 11—then a wave of studies follows; an understandable sequence since events are dramatic in part because they are unexpected. But then there is a predicament: we cannot tell how things have changed because we do not know how they were; and not knowing what has changed and what has not, we are not able to determine why what has happened, happened.

In this study, the sequence was just the opposite. The political upheaval over Muslims and multiculturalism in the Netherlands occurred in 2001; our survey of the concerns and values of the electorate was conducted in 1998. We will show that the strains between Muslims and Western Europeans were evident before the upheaval. The beliefs of each about the other were not a product of September 11—quite the contrary, they provided the basis for reactions to it.

The Netherlands is celebrated for its tolerance, but it has been struggling with the challenge of diversity. We have worked to understand what this struggle teaches about the strengths and limits of liberal democracy. We take advantage of a number of experiments and several thousand interviews to test whether what we believe to be true, is true. But this book is more nearly a diary of walks under the low Dutch sky, with one of us coming to grips emotionally and intellectually with a quandary his country now faces, the other striving to take in what truly was being said. This book is a record of the conclusions we have come to through a long partnership; still more, through a deep friendship.

We have many to thank. For support: to the west of the Atlantic, the National Science Foundation (NSF Grant SR-9515006); to the east, the Dutch National Science Foundation (NWO Grant 510−50−805) and the Dutch Ministry of Public Health, Welfare and Sports. For a month to work together, we gratefully thank the Bellagio Study Center of the Rockefeller Foundation; for help in mounting the study, Shervin Nekuee, Philip Tetlock, and Oliver John; for help in analysis, José Pepels and Matthew Levendusky, and, for getting us through an especially perplexing problem, Jed Stiglitz. We again owe thanks to our partner, Tom Piazza, as does everyone who subsequently will make use of this data set, for doing all that is necessary—and it is a great deal—to archive this data set. Among the colleagues we are indebted to: Pierangelo Peri for the benefit of his expertise on Italy; Maykel Verkuyten for his detailed comments on the manuscript and invaluable suggestions for improving it; Peer Scheepers for his encouragement and advice; Karen Phalet for her generosity in making available her data set on Muslims in the Netherlands; and Alena Kantorová for her encouragement and suggestions for our research. At Stanford we have two institutional debts. We thank the Freeman Spogli Institute for International Studies and particularly the Hoover Institution for support when it was most needed. We also have two personal debts: to Karen Cook, then dean of social sciences, for rescuing the sabbatical of one of us; and to Rob Reich, a colleague in the department, for performing a comparable intellectual rescue of both of us.

We have attempted to write a book one might read for the pleasure of reading it. We certainly have not succeeded. But we have come much closer to success thanks to a quartet of friends—Grant Barnes, John Cardoza, Martin Shapiro, and Barbara Wolfinger. Finally, we are indebted to Chuck Myers, a paradigm of an editor.

Then, as always, there is Suzie.

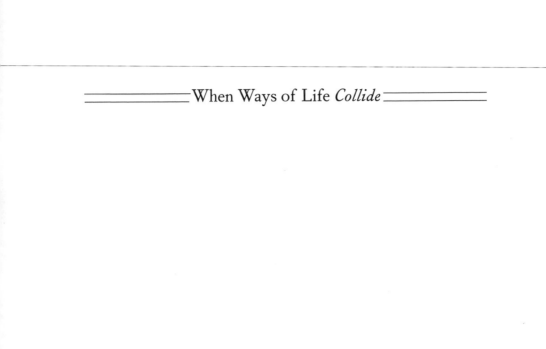

When Ways of Life *Collide*

CHAPTER I

Introduction

THIS IS A BOOK about a vulnerability of liberal democracy. The subject is the incorporation of immigrant minorities in Western Europe. The issue is multiculturalism.

It is a story of ironies from the beginning. The argument for multiculturalism now is made on grounds of principle, but the policy originally was adopted out of convenience. The assumption was that immigrants would be needed for the economy for only a short while. Then they would (and should) leave. Their ties to the country and culture they came from, therefore, should be maintained. Hence the government programs to sustain the culture of minority immigrants—to ensure, for example, that they continued to speak the language of the country they came from, even if they did not master the one they were in. The objective was to equip them to leave—which is to say, to discourage them from staying.[1]

A decade later, as though it were quite natural, a policy that began with one aim was committed to the opposite one. The government redoubled its efforts to support traditional institutions and values of immigrants, not to equip them to return to their former country but to embed them in their new one. Multiculturalism had taken off. Principle had become the driving force, with costs or risks a secondary consideration, when a consideration at all. The countries that have made the most ambitious commitment to multiculturalism, the Netherlands and Great Britain, made the commitment first; they debated

---

[1] See, for example, Entzinger and Beizeveld 2003; Hagendoorn, Veenman, and Vollebergh 2003a.

the consequences only later. Informed circles agreed until recently that multiculturalism was the right policy—right as a matter of effective public policy, but above all right morally.

It is easy to see why. Large-scale immigration of cultural minorities was underway throughout Western Europe. Cultural diversity was a fact of life. Those responsible for political and social institutions had to deal with a host of immediate problems. Race riots were the most threatening, although not necessarily the most urgent. The conditions of life for immigrants in the early years were appalling; and the intolerance that welcomed them was rightly seen in the context of recent history. The Holocaust had taken place in the lifetime of many who now had responsibility for the political and economic institutions of liberal democracy. Against this background, to oppose multiculturalism was to demonstrate a lack of humanity. It was not merely a moral duty to combat prejudice against disadvantaged minorities; it was a badge of honor.

Prejudice *is* a powerful force behind opposition to multiculturalism. But opposition to multiculturalism is not the same as intolerance. Paradoxically, multiculturalism now is being challenged from opposing sides in Western European democracies—from those at their periphery because they are not committed to the values of liberal democracy, and from those at their center because they are committed to them. This study is an effort to understand why.

ONE VIEW OF THE ISSUE

Ayaan Hirsi Ali was born in 1969 in Mogadishu Somalia as the daughter of Hirsi Magan. When she was twenty-two, her parents arranged a marriage to a Somalian nephew in Canada. Her story is that on her way to Canada, she made her escape to the Netherlands and abandoned her faith, becoming a critic of Muslim treatment of women in the Netherlands.[2] In all its variants, multiculturalism is committed to

---

[2] See Ali 2002, 7–18. This is Hirsi Ali's version of her story, which became disputed in May 2006 when a wider public learned that her real family name was Hirsi Magan.

achieving a greater measure of equality between cultures; but it was precisely a difference in cultures that legitimized the inequality of Muslim women in Western European countries. As a critic of Muslim treatment of women, Ali became a critic of multiculturalism. She achieved prominence almost instantaneously, although not the kind one seeks. After only one appearance on television, Muslim extremists immediately threatened Ali with death.[3] September 11 and the assassinations and mass murders that followed in its wake made all things, if not possible, certainly conceivable. Ayaan Hirsi Ali became the first public figure to go into hiding in the Netherlands since the Nazi persecution of Jews hiding during World War II. She had escaped from a traditional society only to be forced into hiding in a liberal one.

Ali had to hide, but she didn't have to be silent. She made a short film about Muslim women, calling attention to the illiberal aspects of Islam as she perceived them. The movie, *Submission,* which was shown on Dutch television on a late summer night in August 2004, begins by showing a veiled female body overlaid with lines from the Koran—an explicit attack on Muslim fear of female sexuality. *Submission* is a censure of traditional Muslim views of the status of women. One of Ayaan's close friends who assisted her in making the movie was Theo van Gogh. A nephew of the artist Vincent van Gogh, he had a deserved reputation for offensiveness and vulgarity. Van Gogh repeatedly labeled Muslims as people who have intercourse with a species of mountain ram.[4] Following the release of the film, van Gogh was threatened. On an early November morning in 2004, he was shot seven times, stabbed in the chest, and had his throat slit. The assassin turned out to be a young Moroccan man, second generation, well educated, fluent in Dutch. Only a few years earlier he had been featured in a Dutch magazine, his picture on its cover, touted as an example of the success of integrating Muslims into Dutch society.

---

[3] Other Muslims in the Netherlands who had been openly critical of Islam, such as Afshin Ellian, a law professor at the University of Amsterdam, and the writer Hafid Bouazza, also received death threats.

[4] In Dutch, literally "goat fuckers."

Subsequently beset by personal and family difficulties, he had become an affiliate of an international gang of Muslim terrorists.

CONFLICTS

Before September 11, multiculturalism was openly challenged only by political figures on the right—most often the extreme right. Since then, the issue of multiculturalism and Muslims has moved to the center of Western European politics. This is dramatically so in the site of our study, the Netherlands, but it is broadly so throughout Western Europe. It would seem obvious that the strains over Muslims and multiculturalism follow from September 11 and its consequences. We shall show, however, that the fundamental divisions were there before September 11; which is also to say, not because of September 11.

This is a study of a tangle of conflicts: over tolerance, identity, the role of elites in liberal democracies, and even the values of liberal democracy. All were apparent before September 11.

The first line of conflict—between the tolerant and the intolerant—is so much easier to see than the others that it has seemed to many thoughtful people to be the heart—even the whole—of the problem. In Western Europe, as everywhere, a substantial portion of society is prejudiced. They have a litany of complaints about minorities—and not just about this or that minority but about one minority after another. Their prejudice gives them a political rudder to steer by. They do not need to know policy details. All they need to know is how they feel about minorities. The more they dislike them, the more likely they are to reject policies that help them and to support those that exclude them.

It would be foolish to overlook the persisting power of prejudice. But it would be nearly as serious a mistake to underestimate the power of liberal democracies in containing it politically. That is partly because the most susceptible to prejudice in a liberal democracy are those who are at its margins socially and politically. They dislike minorities because they themselves are poor and poorly educated. But because they are poor and poorly educated, they are less likely to act politically on their prejudices; even when they do, they are less likely to be politically influential than their fellow citizens at the center of society. More is at work than prejudice in popular reactions to multiculturalism.

People cannot flourish, the argument for multiculturalism runs, unless they can become who they truly and fully are. They—we—are not isolated atoms, each complete by himself or herself. We belong to larger communities, each with its customs, accomplishments, memories of what was, and images of what should be. For people to realize their full worth, they must appreciate the worth of their collective identity; still more, the culture they live in must recognize the full worth of their collective identity.[5] But ethnic and religious immigrants in Western Europe live in societies that historically have not valued their cultures. The larger society is thus obliged to support the institutions symbolizing and sustaining the collective identities of minorities just as it does those symbolizing and sustaining the identity of the majority.

There is a generosity of spirit here. Britain and the Netherlands have promoted multiculturalism to expand opportunities for minorities to enjoy a better life and to win a respected place of their own in their new society. It is all the more unfortunate, as our findings will show, that the outcome has been the opposite—to encourage exclusion rather than inclusion. The policy put in place to achieve conciliation has created division—certainly of majority against minority, perhaps also of minority against majority.[6] The question is why.

Multiculturalism, like Joseph's coat of many colors, comes in many variations.[7] But in one degree or another, they strive to call attention to differences and to minimize the overlap between them.[8] To some degree this is true for all minorities, but it is true in the highest degree for Muslims, since the points of difference are so visible and go so deep.

---

[5] Taylor 1994. For an empirical account, see Phalet and Swyngedouw 2004.

[6] See Verkuyten and Zaremba 2006.

[7] For a nuanced and gracefully presented analysis of multiculturalism in the chief form it presents itself in the United States, see Reich 2002.

[8] See Arends-Tóth and Van De Vijver 2003; Verkuyten 2005; Verkuyten and Yildiz 2006.

What are the consequences of making issues of cultural and national identity a focal point of political argument? We had a good idea about one consequence before we began this study, and no idea at all about the second. The consequence we anticipated was this: To the extent that members of the majority attach importance to their national identity, the more likely they will be to perceive *their* cultural identity to be threatened. In turn, perceiving minorities as threatening, they reject them.[9] We shall show that both components are true. Valuing a collective identity increases the likelihood of seeing it threatened; seeing it threatened increases the likelihood the majority will reject the minority. This is an important result but not a surprising one. It signals that there is a constituency that can be galvanized in opposition to immigrant minorities. Although public opinion studies can only be suggestive, we shall present results indicating that this constituency is a large one.

The second consequence of making issues of identity a focal point of political argument, the one we had not anticipated, reveals more fully the risk of identity politics. Just as it is true that some people are more concerned about a threat to their cultural identity than others, it is also true that the same person can be more concerned about such a threat in some circumstances than in others. It is obvious how people who perceive a threat will respond when issues of cultural identity are brought to the fore. It is by no means obvious how people who do not believe that there is a threat to the national culture will respond.

Here are two scenarios. In the first, when politicians bring issues of collective identity to the fore, it sparks a reaction among those already concerned about issues of identity. In the second, it also sparks a reaction among those who ordinarily are not concerned about issues of identity.

The politics of the two scenarios differ profoundly. To the degree the first applies, it is relatively easy on the one hand for political leaders to evoke an anti-immigrant reaction from those already predisposed against immigrants but difficult for them to do more. To the de-

---

[9] For the most thoughtful exposition of this "individual differences" approach, see Huddy 2001. See also Oakes 2002; and Huddy 2002.

gree the second scenario applies, it is easier for political leaders to break out of the core constituency concerned with issues of identity and provoke exclusionary reactions in the electorate as a whole.

Which scenario better captures the dynamic of identity politics in Western Europe? We carried out special purpose experiments to observe how ordinary citizens respond when issues of national or cultural identity become salient. The experiments are designed to answer two questions that are worth distinguishing. The first has to do with *how easily* an exclusionary reaction can be elicited. It is one thing for people to react negatively to minorities when a spotlight is trained on issues of identity or when the institutions and values of their society are openly threatened. It is another thing for them to react to just a word or phrase. The second has to do with *how* wide the circle is in the larger society that reacts when their national identity is made salient. Obviously, those at the periphery of society will react. But what about those at its center? They are markedly more tolerant and markedly less likely to believe that the majority culture is threatened. And yet, as we shall see, they, too, can be brought into the circle of opposition by making collective identities salient.

Of course, a reaction can be evoked from virtually anyone in extreme circumstances. When a bank robber waving a shotgun tells customers in the bank to raise their hands, everyone's hands go up. Our experimental strategy was just the opposite. Rather than hitting people over the head with a hammer, we aimed, as it were, to brush against them with a feather. To be able to provoke a reaction with modest experimental "manipulations" points to an underlying sensitivity to issues of national and cultural identity; still more, it points to a capacity to mobilize support for exclusionary reactions to immigrants in the electorate as a whole, not just in the segment already concerned about threats to cultural or national identity.

It is eerie, for us, to write these words. Four years after we did our study, the political landscape in the Netherlands was turned upside down by a charismatic figure campaigning against multiculturalism. Of course, our findings did not "predict" this. But they do point to the "flash" potential of identity politics—the speed with which large numbers can be mobilized in opposition to multiculturalism. There is, we fear, a bitter irony here. Striving in the fashion that political leaders have to spotlight and honor differences in the culture and values of majority and minority, they have evoked the very exclusionary reaction they meant to avoid—and what is more, evoked it from those who otherwise would not have been concerned about differences in identity.

POLITICAL LEADERS AND THE ELECTORATE

Citizens only get to choose from the choices offered. Beginning in the 1980s a consensus among political elites developed on multiculturalism—more exactly, a consensus in some countries in Western Europe embedded in a larger antiracism consensus in all. The fact of consensus itself became one more reason for still more consensus. The more who identified racism with opposition to multiculturalism, the fewer who would openly criticize it and the more complete the consensus would appear to be. Periodic examples of public figures whose careers were damaged, or ended, by public statements that were construed as "insensitive" made sure the lesson of political correctness was well learned.

Of course, some disagreed. But it was not necessary to think that encouraging multiculturalism was the right thing to do, only that contesting it was the wrong thing to do. The center-left wanted to promote diversity; the center-right wanted to avoid backlash. So in Great Britain and the Netherlands, the mainstream party of the left sponsored multiculturalism, while the mainstream party of the right acquiesced in it. Together, the programmatic convictions of the one and the principled acquiescence of the other removed the issue of multiculturalism from electoral politics.

This cross-party consensus turned the politics of tolerance upside down. When parties compete, politics operates bottom up with political leaders responding to electoral pressures from below. When they collude, it operates top down with elites in control of the public agenda and thus able to remove some issues from contention. But politicians have means other than agenda control to exert influence. We want to bring to light one of them, not the most important but possibly the most intriguing—namely, conformity pressures. There is, we shall show, a paradox. On the one hand, the more importance that people attach to conformity as a social value, the more likely they are to oppose multiculturalism. On the other hand, the more importance they attach to conformity, the more susceptible they are to social pressure. The result for party leaders on both left and right is the same: that part of their constituency most likely to oppose multiculturalism is the same part whose opposition is most easy to contain.

CONFLICTS OF VALUES

Finally, there is the conflict between Western European and Muslim values. In some ways, it is the most obvious aspect of the current situation; in others, the most elusive: obvious because there is a collision of values; elusive because, for reasons not immediately obvious, this collision of values need not entail conflict.

This collision of values gives currency to a phrase of the day: "the conflict of civilizations." Conflict on this scale, however, is not what we have in mind. To speak of a conflict of civilizations suggests that the points of difference are comprehensive and the conflict irreconcilable. We do not believe either applies here. When we speak of ways of life colliding, we have in mind genuine differences about what is right and wrong embedded in a larger context of common ground. The points of difference, though sharp, are limited; the area of agreement, though not complete, is large. The points of conflict go to both groups' understanding of their way of life; and because they concern not what people think about abstract principles but what choices they make—indeed, cannot avoid making—in their everyday lives, the points of difference cut deep.

It is a truism that a conflict of values leads to conflict between groups and, if a conflict already exists, aggravates it. It is all the more interesting, then, that this is a truism that is false. There is a collision of values: Western Europeans take exception to Muslim treatment of women and children; Muslims to Western European treatment of women and children. The Muslim minority is in no position to demand that the majority conform to their values. The majority is in a position to de-mand the minority conform to theirs. It is only reasonable to suppose that they will do so. Reasonable but, as we shall show, wrong. Many Dutch take strong exception to Muslim practices but have a positive attitude toward Muslims themselves. They are as supportive of the right of Muslims to follow their own way of life in the Netherlands as those who have a positive attitude toward Muslims in all respects.

We readily acknowledge that there is an obvious objection. There is no reason to doubt that that the Dutch mean what they say when they say they dislike the way Muslim men treat Muslim women and the way Muslim parents treat their children. There is some reason, however, to doubt that they mean what they say when they say they like Muslims themselves. After all, they may be saying not what they believe but what they think they are supposed to believe.

This objection has to be right: some people who say nice things about minorities can't stand them. The question, though, is not whether there are some people like this but whether those who say they object to Muslim treatment of women and children not out of prejudice but from principle in the largest number mean what they say. Acknowledging that in the end one cannot prove a negative, we accept the burden of proof. We will go to some lengths to test whether those who say they like Muslims, although they strongly dis-like their treatment of women and children, are being sincere.

We accept the burden of proof because there is a deep misunder-standing of the value of tolerance—about its character and power—among those most concerned about issues of tolerance. They under-stand it to be a negative disposition—a willingness to put up with an-other individual or group even though you dislike or disagree with them. It makes sense to think of tolerance requiring people to jump a hurdle to be in a position to be tolerant, if what you have in mind is political tolerance. How can you tell if someone is tolerant if you only ask him if people he agrees with should have the right to express their point of view? Surely the test of tolerance is the willingness to sup-port the right of people you disagree with, even possibly detest, to ex-press *their* point of view. But we are concerned with another kind of tolerance—social, not political.

The two are quite different. What sense does it make to argue that you can only be in a position to be tolerant of, say, Jews, if you dislike them? If you have to dislike or disagree with a group in order to be in a position to be tolerant of it, then only anti-Semites are in a position to be tolerant of Jews. Social tolerance requires more than political tolerance. It is not enough to be willing to put up with a minority group. At a minimum, it is necessary that one not dislike and reject others because they belong to another ethnic, religious, or racial group. But tolerance does not stop with neutrality. To be truly tolerant, one must be ready to accept others, to think well of them, and to be well disposed toward them.

What is at stake is not a disagreement over definitions. The issue is whether, in real life, a deep conflict of values leads a majority to reject a minority. That value conflict exacerbates group conflict is the obvious expectation; it certainly was our expectation. But like so many others, we underestimated the power of tolerance. Those who believe there is a conflict between Western European and Muslim values, but who nonetheless have a positive view of Muslims, are as supportive of the right of Muslim immigrants to follow their own way of life in the Netherlands as those who reject the idea that there is a conflict of values.

The fundamental issue, it turns out, is not diversity but loyalty. Do Muslim minorities want to adopt the country they have come to and its core values as theirs? Or do they want to live in it, but not be a part of it, reserving their fundamental loyalty for the country they came from and its culture and institutions? They are questions that cut deep. Many, including many of the most tolerant, believe that Muslim immigrants continue to give their loyalty to the country they came from, not the country they have come to. Among the many ironies of our story, this is perhaps the most gratuitous. Multiculturalism encouraged an ambiguity of commitment. On the one side, political and intellectual elites ruled out a declaration of identification with the larger society as inappropriate. On the other side, Muslim leaders have acted as though identification with the larger society was unnecessary. Both could have made different choices; if either had, there well may not have been a pervasive suspicion about the loyalty of the Muslim community as a whole *before* the overt demonstration of disloyalty of a few.

THE SITE OF OUR STUDY

"God created the world, but the Dutch created the Netherlands" goes a popular Dutch saying. Much of the Netherlands is surrounded by water, and a large part of it would be underwater but for the creation of dykes. The distances are small; it takes less than two hours by car to cross the country from east to west, and about three hours to cross it from north to south. The opposite side of the coin is that the population density is the highest in Europe and among the highest in the world.

The Netherlands is also a country with a tradition of tolerance. As early as the seventeenth century, Amsterdam was a popular capital in Europe, partly because of its liberal and tolerant climate, still more because of its "embarrassment of riches," as Schama has characterized it.[10] Certainly because of the first, and possibly because of the second, the Netherlands offered asylum to religious and political refugees who could find protection from persecution and enjoy freedom of thought and belief. Thus the image of the Netherlands as a tolerant country came into being. It is now known for more contemporary forms of tolerance—coffee shops selling soft drugs, legal prostitution, euthanasia, and gay marriage.

The Netherlands historically has been a country of emigration, albeit one with a tradition of immigration: rich Protestants from the southern Dutch provinces during the Eighty Years' War; German seasonal workers since the sixteenth century; Jews after 1619; and French Huguenots at the end of the seventeenth century. Gypsies moved in and out throughout this whole period.[11] The twentieth century witnessed the arrival of yet other foreign populations. In the 1920s groups of Chinese laid off by Dutch steamships settled in Rotterdam and Amsterdam.[12] In the 1950s about 40,000 South Moluccans[13] together with some 200,000 Indo-Dutch "returned" with the

[10] Schama 1987.

[11] Tanja 1987; Lucassen 1987.

[12] Dubbelman and Tanja 1987.

[13] The Moluccans are a group of islands in Indonesia.

Dutch colonial army after the declaration of independence of the state of Indonesia, a late Dutch colony. The 1960s in turn welcomed some smaller groups of Italian, Spanish, and Yugoslav labor immigrants.

All the same, the real reversal from a country of emigration to an immigration country—although this was never officially admitted—occurred in the 1970s. Responding to a shortage of unskilled labor in the 1970s, the government approved of and assisted in labor recruitment in Morocco, in North Africa, and Turkey in the Middle East. Almost simultaneously Surinamese and Antilleans emigrated to the Netherlands from the Caribbean Dutch colonies. In addition, refugees from Sri Lanka, Iran, Iraq, Somalia, and other African countries streamed into the Netherlands in the 1980s and 1990s, while at the same time the Turkish and Moroccan groups further grew as relatives joined family members already in the Netherlands. Currently about 2.6 million people in the Netherlands qualify as immigrants by their birth or that of one of their parents. Most broadly defined, some 17 percent of the Dutch population is of foreign descent. The largest groups are the Surinamese, Turks, and Moroccans, each numbering between 225,000 and 300,000, and the Antilleans, which number about 100,000. Refugees number about 150,000, and other smaller groups include Moluccans and Southern Europeans.[14] The prognosis is that Muslims will outnumber the Dutch in the three largest cities in the Netherlands within the decade. All are less well-off than the native Dutch. But of the four largest groups, the Muslims, the Turks, and the Moroccans are the least well-off.

The Netherlands has always been a country of minorities thanks to the power of religion to divide as well as unite.[15] The southern part of the country is traditionally Roman Catholic and the northern part is traditionally Protestant, the latter being further divided into Lutheran, Reformed, and Dutch Reformed. These religious differences were institutionalized in the separate—or "pillarized"—state structures: parallel labor unions, employers unions, newspapers, broad-

---

[14] Hagendoorn, Veenman, and Vollebergh 2003b.

[15] Andeweg and Irwin 2003, 229–40.

casting stations, medical care organizations, and even universities for Protestants and Roman Catholics.[16]

This pillarized system collapsed toward the end of the 1960s, partly as a result of increasing secularization of the Dutch society, partly as a result of increasing social as well as geographic mobility. Still, given this history of segmentation, it is not surprising that the party system remains complex. The principal party of the left is the Social Democratic Party (PvdA, Partij van de Arbeid), with two somewhat more radical parties to its left, the Greens (Groen Links) and the Socialists (SP, Socialistische Partij). The principal party of the right is the VVD (Partij voor Vrijheid en Democratie), or the Conservative Liberal Party. In between is D'66 (Democraten '66) and the fragments of the traditional Christian parties now united in the Christian Democratic Party (CDA, Christen Democratisch Appel). The Social Democrats favor policies to reduce both economic and social inequality. The Liberal Party, while supportive of policies to reduce economic inequality and provide social welfare, is not supportive of policies to reduce social inequality and has more of a market orientation to the economy, though the difference is one of degree, not kind. The Christian Democrats focus their appeal on support for traditional values—expressed in antifeminist, anti-euthanasia, and anti-abortion policies.[17]

It is, on the one hand, a complex system; on the other hand, it is a surprisingly simple one. The number of parties makes coalition government inescapable; the broad support for a culture of egalitarianism makes possible coalitions that might seem impossible. Thus, the principal party of the left, the Social Democrats, joined hands with the principal party of the right, the Liberals in the 1990s. This coalition allowed the government to negotiate a series of consecutive "gentlemen's agreements" between labor unions and employers, restraining rising salaries in return for low inflation and employment.

---

[16] The seminal account of a "consociational" structure of democratic politics is Lijphart 1977. For a comprehensive account and analysis of recent Dutch politics, see Andeweg and Irwin 2003.

[17] Andeweg and Irwin 1993, 102.

The result: the "Dutch Miracle" of unprecedented economic growth in the late 1990s.[18]

Politically, the Dutch have a collective trauma. The German occupation during World War II stands out as a period of extraordinary humiliation. The institutionalized Dutch memory is that they, the Dutch, failed to resist the German occupiers as they should have—still more, failed to resist the deportation of Dutch Jews as they should have. It cannot be surprising that immigrant minorities have been seen in the light of the Holocaust—powerless and dependent, deserving the help and protection of the Dutch—or that critical views of immigrants are labeled racist and xenophobic. A societal consensus, at the elite level, was formed in support of multiculturalism—and not just of a symbolic variety. In the Netherlands, as much as can be done on behalf of multiculturalism has been done. Minority groups are provided instruction in their own language and culture; separate radio and television programs; government funding to import religious leaders; and subsidies for a wide range of social and religious organizations; "consultation prerogatives" for community leaders; and publicly financed housing set aside for and specifically designed to meet Muslim requirements for strict separation of "public" and "private" spaces.[19]

In the 1990s, as the multiculturalism program took root, the Netherlands became an increasingly wealthy country. The average income was high, though the taxes were as well. A large part of the income was redistributed through an intricate system of social welfare that had been gradually built in the 1950s and 1960s. It was designed to protect the Dutch against unemployment, illness, and old age and is in sharp contrast to the thin Anglo-Saxon welfare model in Britain and the United States. Unfortunately, the simultaneous exhaustion of natural gas reserves and the expense of so extensive a welfare state required drastic expenditure cuts in the 1980s to lower the government deficit. The result: private wealth and public decay, tight purse strings in the economic realm and unbounded ambitiousness in the cultural.

---

[18] Visser and Hemerijck 1997.

[19] Koopmans 2005.

OUR CLAIM

It is necessary, proponents of multiculturalism contend, to go beyond "mere" tolerance because the heart of the matter is that the majority honor the claims of minorities to their own identities. This ordering of tolerance and identity, we will argue, gets things wrong all the way down. Bringing issues of collective identity to the fore undercuts support for the right of ethnic and religious minorities to follow their own ways of life. Tolerance, not identity, provides the foundation for diversity.

CHAPTER 2

Muslims

THIS IS A BOOK about issues of diversity and tolerance in the Netherlands. An odd choice, you may think—a country too far away to be of interest to Americans, too small to be of importance to Europeans, and a country in any case famous for its tolerance. Yet it turned out to be the best possible choice. It was in the Netherlands that the politics of multiculturalism erupted.

POLITICAL FIRESTORM

Prior to the 1960s Dutch society was divided—one set of school systems, unions, mass media, political parties, and sports clubs for Protestants; a parallel set for Catholics and another nonconfessionals—with the government funding all. Catholic, Protestant, and nonconfessional communities lived independent of one other; their leaders, however, consulted and coordinated with one another behind closed doors.[1] Separation and the assertion of autonomy at the level of citizens, cooperation and collusion at the level of politicians—two planes of politics that rarely intersected.

The so-called system of pillarization gave way in the face of secularization in the 1960s. But consultative politics among leaders in back rooms continued; indeed, it was extended. Through the 1970s and 1980s, the Christian Democrats held the balance of power, sometimes siding with the party of the center-left, the Social Democrats (PvdA),

---

[1] In Dutch, *Achterkamertjespolitiek*; see Andeweg and Irwin 2003, 229–40.

sometimes with the party of the right, the Conservative Liberals (VVD). In 1994, the historical opponents, the Social Democrats and the Conservatives, joined together, excluding the Christian Democrats and forming the Purple Coalition.[2]

It was called the Purple Coalition because purple stands for the merger of the red of social democracy with the blue of liberal conservatism. The left agreed to the lowering of the state debt; the right to the maintenance of the central aspects of the welfare system; and both right and left agreed on the priority of reducing unemployment. The main aim of the Purple Coalition was to escape from the cycle of state debt, inflation, and unemployment. In its economic program, the coalition was extremely successful.

It also continued to promote the most ambitious program of multiculturalism in Western Europe.[3] The state funds a Muslim school system in which children are taught in the language of their country of origin and, in an independently designed curriculum, about their own culture. The state also builds separate Muslim housing; provides mass media (including radio and television) dedicated to Muslim interests and concerns; imports imams; supports separate social and welfare arrangements for immigrant minorities; and has established a separate consultation system with community "leaders."

With the political right and left joining hands over multiculturalism, there was no political opening for citizens to express discontent. But a vacuum is hard to maintain in politics. Then again, considering what happened, a more apt metaphor may be dry tinder and a fiery spark.

The Purple Coalition produced enormous private wealth at the expense of public services. Hospitals had long waiting lists because of budgetary restrictions; schools and police services had been centralized to cut costs, leaving masses of pupils and citizens feeling anonymous and alienated; immigrants had been located in the poor neighborhoods

[2] Left Liberals of D'66 participated as a junior partner.

[3] See Koopmans et al. 2005. At the same time, in the way of politics, Dutch policy is committed to "integration," which includes, among other things, passage of the Dutch Citizenship Law requiring a demonstration of oral and written knowledge of Dutch and knowledge of Dutch history. See also Entzinger and Beizeveld 2003.

of the cities then—in one of the many ironies of multiculturalism—
left alone to solve their problems because they were an independent
community. These were, in the phrase of the day, the "ruins" of the
Purple Coalition.

Pim Fortuyn stepped forward as a critic of the "ruins," still more so
as a critic of multiculturalism. Multiculturalism was the issue that divided Fortuyn most deeply from established political elites. Concern
had been growing in the general public about the ballooning number
of immigrants and the social problems that followed in their train—
crime, disproportionate numbers of immigrant women seeking refuge
in battered women's shelters, immigrants unemployed and on social
welfare, and immigrants in prison. But Fortuyn's criticism of multiculturalism went deeper. Multiculturalism, he charged, legitimized
repressive practices of Islam; indeed, it propped them up financially.

Some of life's ironies are unavoidable; this was not one of them.
The Dutch government funded the immigration of imams, princi-
pally from Turkey and Morocco. They were selected for their piety,
not the breadth of their experience. They were thus simultaneously
erudite and ignorant. They knew everything about the Koran but
nothing about the Netherlands. They were nuanced in their traditional Hadith interpretations but blind to the moral complications of
living a modern Muslim life in Western Europe.

One of their central concerns was (as they saw it) the lust, deca-
dence, homosexuality, and feminism of the West. In the summer of
2001, an imam publicly condemned homosexuality and equated gays
with "pigs." His sermon might ordinarily have been lost in the hub-
bub of ordinary life, but with the sight of the collapse of the Twin
Towers, televised scenes of Moroccan youths cheering the horror,
and the beginning of the War on Terrorism, a man who otherwise
might have been viewed as silly came to be seen as the spearhead of a
fifth column.

Fortuyn insisted the imam had a right to say what he thought. But
he, too, had a right to say what he thought. He, Fortuyn, was gay.
Who was this imam to come to his country to say that he was a
"pig"? Islam, Fortuyn retorted, was "a backward religion"—backward in its intolerance of homosexuals and in its denial of equality

to women.[4] It was Muslims, he insisted, not those who were critical of them, who failed the test of tolerance.

So Fortuyn identified himself with the value of tolerance even as his opponents identified him with intolerance. Nearly all leading figures denounced him as a populist, a fascist, a demagogue. The Left Liberals (D'66) invoked the memory of Anne Frank. The Green Left called Fortuyn "not right wing but *extreme* right-wing."[5] The Social Democrats said, "Now we know what we are against!" and later, "If you wake up in France you see LePen and if you wake up in Holland you see Fortuyn."

Despite this barrage of criticism, and without the backing of an established party organization, he took the lead in election polls. This surge partly reflected his personal appeal.[6] He was a gifted orator: emotional, direct, aggressive on the one hand, friendly and easygoing on the other. Above all, his criticism of multiculturalism struck a chord, not merely among those at the margins of Dutch society but also among those at its center.[7] Fortuyn's party won the election. Fortuyn might well have been prime minister—but he was assassinated nine days before the election.[8] The politics of the Netherlands since then has been the politics of multiculturalism in extremis.

A CONFLICT OF VALUES

When one group of people fails to do what another group of people believes that they should do—still more, when what they actually do is what the other group believes that they should not do—their values collide.

---

[4] Fortuyn used the Dutch word *achterlijk*, which literally means backward but also connotes stupidity.

[5] Van Holsteyn, Irwin, and den Ridder 2003, 71.

[6] A substantial proportion of Fortuyn's electorate were "new voters," people who reported either never to have voted or not to have voted in the previous election. See Van Praag 2003.

[7] See, for example, Van Praag 2003; Van der Brug 2003; and Van Hosteyn, Irwin, and den Ridder 2003.

[8] There is ambiguity about the motive. Initially, the assassin claimed it was in defense of animal rights; subsequently, to protect Muslims. In any case, the assassin was not Muslim.

What are the consequences of a conflict of group values? The answer is surely obvious: The deeper the conflict, the more likely each group is to reject the other. The purpose of this chapter is to bring out why this answer, which appears self-evidently right, in this case is more wrong than right.

The Western European View of Muslims

What matters enough to bring ordinary people into conflict? It is not culture as an abstract noun. The values of a culture come to life in actual practices—in how people treat one another. They encapsulate not merely what people believe but who they are.[9]

Two sources of value conflict between Western Europeans and Muslim immigrants stand out.[10] The first is the status of women in Muslim culture.[11] Turks and Moroccans in the Netherlands come predominantly from the rural areas in Turkey (Anatolia) and Morocco (Rif). In both, Muslim women do not have the same standing as men to choose whom they will marry, to pursue an education, to retain the right to dispose of property they bring to marriage, to pursue a career after marriage, to dress or interact socially, to enter into major decisions of the family, or even to define the terms on which they will engage in sexual relations as men do. Marriages are arranged by the parents, with a preference for endogamous marriage with a parallel cousin (a son or daughter of a father's brother). The marriage relation is officially asymmetrical. The husband is the head of the family and has the duty of protecting the honor of his family; the wife, who most assuredly is not the head of the family, has the duty of obeying her husband.

Then, too, Muslim family relations are markedly more authoritarian than they are among the Dutch. Muslim children tend to be kept under strict surveillance and control. Behavior that is challenging is

[9] Verkuyten 2005.

[10] Van der Hoek 1994; Van den Berg-Eldering 1982.

[11] Muslim culture refers to commonalities in the way of life in countries where the majority are Muslims. One of the crucial differences between Muslim countries and Western countries is the treatment of women. See Buruma and Margalit 2004, 127 (Dutch edition).

punished by threat, verbal violence, or corporal punishment. Girls are even more closely watched than boys, since virginity bears on the honor of the family. They are strictly monitored by their father and brothers; their right to take independent action is largely eliminated; and even their freedom to leave the house is curtailed. For that matter, younger children, both boys and girls, tend to be under the discipline and supervision of older brothers and sisters who have a responsibility to monitor, control, and punish them. From a Dutch perspective, then, Muslim childrearing practices are insular, authoritarian, and insufficiently concerned with the interests of the child.

A number of Dutch object to Muslim treatment of women and childrearing practices not on principle but out of prejudice. Criticism allows them to vent hostility. Although they themselves are illiberal, their criticism of Muslims on the ground that *they* are illiberal is too good an opportunity to pass up. All the same, we expect that a substantial number object to Muslim treatment of women and children for just the opposite set of reasons: not from prejudice but out of a conviction that certain Muslim practices are at odds with the values of Dutch society.

To see if principle as well as prejudice is involved, it is necessary to pick out those who take exception to some Muslim practices without taking exception to Muslims themselves. Accordingly, we designed three questions to gauge global evaluations of Muslims in the Netherlands. The pattern for all three is the same, as table 2.1 shows. Approximately half of our Dutch sample disagree that "Muslims have a lot to offer Dutch culture." Approximately half also agree that "Western European and Muslim ways of life are irreconcilable." And about half disagree that "Most Muslims in the Netherlands respect other cultures." An example of the proverbial half-empty, half-full glass? Not at all. The absolute number of Dutch respondents who express a negative judgment of Muslims demonstrates that there is no shortage of people who dislike Muslims. Still more important is the consistency of criticism: those who criticize Muslims on one ground are markedly likely to criticize them on every other.[12]

---

[12] The median intercorrelation is .4; alpha is .66.

TABLE 2.1
Global Evaluations of Muslims

	Agree strongly (%)	Agree somewhat (%)	Disagree somewhat (%)	Disagree strongly (%)
Muslims have a lot to offer Dutch culture (N = 1876)	14.4	30.9	19.4	35.3
Western European and Muslim ways of life are irreconcilable (N = 1907)	30.5	22.1	20.6	26.9
Most Muslims in the Netherlands respect other cultures (N = 1755)	21.1	30.1	21.8	27.0

A substantial body of the Dutch public has a globally negative view of Muslim immigrants.

We also asked two questions that call not for global assessments of Muslims but for appraisals of specific Muslim practices—notably, Muslim treatment of women and Muslim parents' treatment of their children. The level of agreement among the Dutch is overwhelming, as table 2.2 shows. Approximately nine out of every ten agree that Muslim men in the Netherlands dominate their women; six out of ten agree strongly. The response to childrearing practices is also one-sided. Three out of every four Dutch agree that Muslims in the Netherlands raise their children in an authoritarian way; four out of ten agree strongly.

There is a consensus in Dutch society. Muslims do not treat women or children as they should treat them; more exactly, they treat them as they should *not* treat them.[13]

[13] In a follow-up study, Gijsbers 2005 found that positive views of Muslim contributions to Dutch culture and Muslims' respect for other cultures slipped from approximately 50 percent to approximately 30 percent after four years. As expected, Dutch disagreement with Muslim treatment of women and children held steady. Gijsbers 2005, 189–205.

TABLE 2.2

Evaluations of Muslim Cultural Norms

	Agree strongly	Agree somewhat	Disagree somewhat	Disagree strongly
Muslim men in the Netherlands				
dominate their women	63.9%	25.5%	4.6%	6.0%
(N = 1860)	(1189)	(474)	(85)	(112)
Muslims in the Netherlands				
raise children in an				
authoritarian way	41.3%	34.6%	14.0%	10.1%
(N = 1728)	(714)	(598)	(242)	(174)

A Look in the Mirror: Muslim Evaluations of Western Europeans

A conflict of values is a two-way street. What each thinks is right, the other thinks is wrong. The Dutch disagree with Muslims' treatment of women and children. Do Muslims similarly disagree with Dutch treatment of women and children?

The idea was to ask Muslim immigrants mirror image questions of the ones that we asked Dutch about Muslims.[14] Having asked the Dutch whether Muslims have a lot to offer Dutch culture, we would, for example, ask Muslims whether Western European culture has a lot to offer Islam. An excellent idea, if we say so ourselves. But in social science as in life, there is many a slip between cup and lip. The wording of two of the three global questions in the Muslim survey is similar to that in the Dutch survey; the wording of one dissimilar. More seriously, two of three global questions in the Dutch survey asked whether Muslims had favorable qualities; all three of the global questions in the Muslim survey asked whether Western Europeans had negative qualities. Still more seriously, respondents had an

---

[14] We are grateful to our colleague Karen Phalet, who directed the Muslim Immigrant Study and took the initiative in developing these items. Phalet, VanLotringen, and Entzinger 2000.

"escape" option in the Muslim survey but not in the Dutch. Rather than having to agree or disagree, they could answer "neither agree nor disagree." Not surprisingly, this is the most frequently chosen alternative; regrettably, it is also the most ambiguous. People may say that they neither agree nor disagree because they don't have a view of the matter one way or the other. Or they may say it precisely because they do have a view—a negative one—which they do not wish to voice. To facilitate comparison of Muslim views of Western Europeans with Western Europeans' of Muslims, we present the distribution of answers with the "neither agree, nor disagree" category excluded.[15]

Two samples of Muslim immigrants were drawn—one of Turkish Muslims, the other of Moroccan Muslims. Consider the global evaluations of Turkish Muslims of Western Europeans. Approximately half agree that Western European culture has nothing to contribute to Islam; a similar number agree that Western European history is marked by excessive warfare and violence; a slightly smaller number agree that Western Europeans have no respect for Muslim culture. Approximately the same proportion of Turkish Muslim immigrants, then, agree with global negative evaluations of Western Europeans (although fewer agree strongly) as Western Europeans agree with global negative evaluations of Muslims.

But, one might reply, Turkish immigrants believe what they believe not by virtue of being Muslims but by virtue of being Turks. Here is where having two samples of two different groups of Muslims is far better than having one twice as large of either. Minor points of difference are detectible between Moroccan and Turkish immigrants, as table 2.3 shows. The former are slightly *less* likely than the latter to agree that Western European culture has nothing to contribute to Islam but slightly *more* likely to agree that West European history is marked by excessive warfare and violence and that West Europeans have no respect for Muslim culture. The differences, though, are minor. For all practical purposes, Moroccan immigrants are as likely

---

[15] It is the ratio of positive to negative responses that is of interest; the ratio is of course the same whether the in-between option is included or excluded.

TABLE 2.3

Global Evaluations of Western Europeans

	Agree strongly (%)	Agree somewhat (%)	Disagree somewhat (%)	Disagree strongly (%)
Turkish Muslims (N = 640)				
Western European culture has nothing to contribute to Islam	15.6	30.5	45.9	7.9
West European history is marked by excessive warfare and violence	9.9	40.4	40.1	9.6
West Europeans have no respect for Muslim culture	12.8	29.3	51.5	6.4
Moroccan Muslims (N = 544)				
Western European culture has nothing to contribute to Islam	10.0	27.0	52.9	10.0
West European history is marked by excessive warfare and violence	25.4	44.5	24.2	5.2
West Europeans have no respect for Muslim culture	14.5	34.8	43.3	7.4

as Turkish immigrants to dislike the Dutch, and both are as likely to dislike the Dutch as the Dutch are likely to dislike them. These results suggest that there are parallel barriers of prejudice: a desire of many Western Europeans to hold Muslims at a distance combined with a desire of Muslims to keep their distance.

THE PURITY OF THE OPPRESSED

We are aware that to suggest any parallelism between minority and majority is controversial in some quarters. Some argue that a minority is, as a matter of principle, incapable of prejudice or discrimination against the majority. Here is a textbook example: "[I]t is misleading to suggest that those in subordinate positions discriminate under any conditions . . . even where subordinate group members do have the power to act . . . their actions will be aimed at challenging and dismantling current structures of inequality rather than creating and defending them."[16]

The myth of the moral purity of the oppressed has a distinguished political lineage. It also is as perplexing as it evidently is appealing. It is never made clear why oppression should be good for one's character: why being poor, on top of being poorly educated, not to mention also being poorly treated, should flower into a commitment to equality and tolerance. Falsified on every occasion it has been invoked, it nonetheless *is* invoked on the next.

Perhaps the need and, therefore, the will to believe are too strong. One can *claim* that minorities necessarily aim at "challenging and dismantling current structures of inequality rather than creating and defending them." But the aim of Muslim immigrants is precisely to maintain a "current structure of inequality"—namely, the inequality of women. Perhaps one is supposed to add, "or so it appears from a Western European perspective"—except it is not a matter of appearance. It is a fact that women do not have equality with men in Muslim cultures; and the more traditional the Muslim culture, the greater the inequality between men and women.[17] For that matter, "a commitment to challenging and dismantling current structures of inequality" does not comport with the eruption of anti-Semitism in Muslim communities in Western Europe.[18]

The very idea of using "a commitment to challenging . . . inequal-

[16] Reicher 2004, 932.

[17] Okin 1999.

[18] See, for example, Schoenfeld 2004.

ity" as a standard of political approval for minority cultures has an odd quality. From the perspective of a traditionally observant Muslim, to suggest that there is a need for a justification of their practices, let alone on the grounds that they promote equality, is to get the issue of justification the wrong way about. It is Western European women who are not being treated as they should. As table 2.4 shows, nearly three out of four Muslim immigrants agree that "Western European women have too many rights and liberties." Just as the Dutch believe that Muslim women are allowed to do too little, Muslim immigrants believe that Western European women are allowed to do too much. The same holds for children. The Dutch be-

TABLE 2.4

Muslim Evaluations of Western European Cultural Norms

	Agree strongly (%)	Agree somewhat (%)	Disagree somewhat (%)	Disagree strongly (%)
Turkish Muslims (N = 640)				
Western European women have too many rights and liberties	19.7	51.1	22.1	7.2
Western European youth have too little respect for their parents	27.4	55.3	15.8	1.5
Moroccan Muslims (N = 544)				
Western European women have too many rights and liberties	24.6	51.2	18.5	5.7
Western European youth have too little respect for their parents	16.2	45.4	18.5	8.2

lieve that Muslim parents treat their children in an authoritarian way. Muslim immigrants see it just the other way around. "Western European youth," they believe, "have too little respect for their parents." It is like looking in a mirror, and seeing your right ear, as it were, on the left, your left ear on the right.

In the stock sermon, misperception is a root cause of group conflict. If only people in one group could see past their stereotypes of those in the other group, the strains between them would ease. This is no doubt true on some occasions but not on this one. Each believes that what the other believes is right, is wrong: and each is right about what the other believes is right—Dutch about Muslims, Muslims about Dutch.

There is a new variation on the stock sermon on group conflict. On the new view, the problem is not that one group misunderstands the culture of another. The problem instead is that it is a misunderstanding to suppose that there is a culture, a definite set of beliefs and values, to be understood. Each culture, the argument runs, is shot through with tensions and contradictions and variations—over time, from place to place, even at the same time and place. Like most arguments about culture, this one comes in different dosages. At the strongest, the claim is that even to speak of "the" culture of another is to fall into "a poor man's sociology"[19]—a nicely patronizing phrase for an argument meant to combat a patronizing view of the thinking of others.

If this view of each culture as pluralistic down to its roots is right, our view of value conflict is wrong. But because many matters of culture resist generalization or require qualification, it does not follow that the values of one cannot conflict with those of another. A Dutch observer can see that women in a Muslim community do not enjoy the same status as women in a Dutch community. A Muslim observer can see that Dutch women have essentially the same freedoms as Dutch men. Muslim immigrants know that the Dutch reject some of their values; the Dutch know that Muslim immigrants reject some of theirs.

[19] An articulate exponent of this view is Benhabib 2002a, 2002b.

VALUE CONFLICT AND PUBLIC POLICY

The most immediate public issue regarding immigrants that public opinion has the power to influence is immigration policy;[20] the most obvious expectation is that the clash of Western European and Muslim values increases opposition to immigration.

Oddly, the exact meaning of this obvious expectation is not obvious. One possibility is that the clash of values has a bigger impact the more people dislike Muslims in general. On this view, disliking Muslim treatment of women and children is like adding fuel to the fire of disliking Muslims in general. The other possibility is that the process works the other way around: disliking Muslim treatment of women and children makes more of a difference for those who like Muslims in general—that is, for those who otherwise would not be inclined to oppose further immigration. If the first view is right, the chief impact of a conflict of values is to increase the likelihood of opposition to immigration on the part of those who already are likely to oppose continued immigration. If the second view is right, the chief impact of value conflict is to increase the likelihood of opposition outside the hard core of those who dislike Muslims pure and simple.

Which view is right matters politically. Those who dislike Muslims pure and simple are concentrated at the periphery of society. The very factors that render them susceptible to prejudice—being poorly educated and poorly off, for example—also make them more likely to be politically marginal. They pay little attention to politics, because they are poorly educated, and they take little part in it, because they are both poorly educated and poorly off. By contrast, those who object to Muslim treatment of women and children but not to Muslims themselves tend to be concentrated at the center of Dutch society. They are not the best off but among the best off; not the most educated but among the most educated; not the highest in occupational status but among the highest.[21] As against those who dislike Muslims pure and simple, they accordingly are more likely to express their

[20] See, for example, Fetzer 2000.
[21] Data are available on request.

views politically; and more political weight is likely to be attached to their views because they are more likely to act on them.

Does a conflict of values chiefly increase opposition among those already predisposed to oppose immigration? Or does it mainly increase opposition among those who otherwise might support it? The probability of making immigration more difficult is plotted on the vertical axis of figure 2.1: the higher the line, the more probable support for making it more difficult. The degree to which respondents dislike Muslims pure and simple is plotted along the horizontal axis: the further to the right, the greater the dislike. The dotted line describes the reactions of those most opposed to Muslim treatment of women and children, the solid line those most approving. The shaded areas indicate the confidence intervals around the estimates.

As a glance shows, the solid line climbs steeply from left to right. No surprise here: dislike for Muslims is a potent inducement in and of itself to oppose immigration. The two curves diverge as you look from right to left, that is, as attention turns from those who dislike Muslims to those who like them. At the far left, the solid line is much

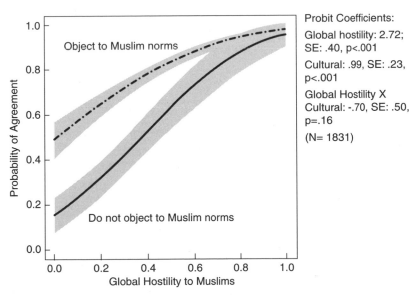

Fig. 2.1. "Immigration should be made more difficult"

lower than the dotted one. The figure shows that only one out of ten who have the most positive attitudes toward Muslims favor making immigration more difficult. By contrast, approximately one out of two who object to Muslim treatment of women and children do. In short, a dislike of some Muslim social practices, quite apart from a dislike of Muslims themselves, contributes to a politically overwhelming level of support in the society as a whole to putting up higher barriers to immigrants.

Here is an irony to savor. Advocates of multiculturalism have worked to rule critical judgments of cultural practices of minority groups out of bounds. This prohibition is meant to benefit minorities. So it may in the short run. But in an only a slightly longer run, our results suggest, it may work just the other way around. On the one side, ruling critical judgments out of bounds reduces incentives for a minority to minimize conflicts of values with a majority. On the other side, it reduces hope among the majority that points of difference will be minimized over time. Ruling critical judgments of particular practices of minorities out of bounds for public discussion may be good fortune for those who already have immigrated. To the degree it increases opposition to further immigration, however, it comes at the expense of those in less fortunate countries who remain in need of an opportunity to emigrate to more fortunate ones.

PRINCIPLE OR PREJUDICE?

But how seriously should we take these results that suggest there is opposition to more minorities because of a principled opposition to some social practices of minorities? How credible is it that Dutch who say they dislike Muslims' denial of equality to women but not Muslims in general are not in fact objecting because, in truth, they really do dislike Muslims? They *say* that they object to Muslim treatment of women out of a commitment to equality. They *say* that they object to Muslim parents' treatment of children out of opposition to authoritarian values. But why take what they say at face value? People can always find a high-minded reason for disliking another group.

In the right circumstances, nearly all of us are tempted to present touched-up portraits of ourselves—ones that bring out our more attractive features and put our less attractive ones in the shadow. But how is it possible to tell whether prejudice is lurking behind a profession of high-minded principles?

What we need is a secret measure of prejudice, as it were: a way to persuade the people we interview that they can express a negative reaction to minorities without our knowing that they are doing so. The list experiment was devised to observe how people respond when they believe that no can observe how they respond.[22] Here is the way it works. A random sample is randomly divided into halves. One half is assigned to the "baseline" condition, the other half to the "test" condition. In the baseline condition, the interviewer begins by announcing, "I'm going to read you a list of some things that make some people angry. I want you to tell me how many make you angry or upset. I don't want you to tell me *which ones,* just *how many.*" Then the interviewer reads a list of items—children in a museum, the income of professional soccer players; advertisements on television; shops open on Sunday. In the test condition almost everything is the same. The interviewer again says, "I'm going to read you a list of some things that make some people angry. I want you to tell me how many make you angry or upset. I don't want you to tell me *which ones,* just *how many.*" Again she lists children in a museum; the income of professional soccer players; advertisements on television; shops open on Sunday. There is just one difference: In the test condition, there is an additional item—special assistance for minorities.

Suppose we are interviewing a respondent in the test condition. Suppose also that this particular respondent is vexed by children in the museum and greatly dislikes assistance for minorities. He then is asked: How many make you angry? Not which ones, just how many? He answers, two. Now, he knows that there is no way that the interviewer can figure out that one of the two that make him angry is

---

[22] Kuklinski devised the list technique and has done extensive validity studies. See Kuklinski and Cobb 1998; Gilens, Sniderman, and Kuklinski 1998; Kuklinski, Cobb, and Gilens, 1997; Kuklinski et al. 1997.

assistance for minorities. He knows this because the list is five items long.[23] So he can express anger toward minorities without the interviewer's being able to tell that he is doing so.

And he is right. The interviewer has no way to figure out that one of the two angry responses refers to minorities. But the data analyst can easily figure it out. To know the proportion angry at assistance for minorities, it only is necessary to calculate the mean number of angry responses in the baseline condition, subtract it from the mean number of angry responses in the test condition, then multiply by 100. The data analyst will not know the particular individuals who are angry. But she will be able to identify characteristics of individuals—for example, their view of Muslim treatment of women and children—that increase (or decrease) the proportion angry over assistance for minorities. The list experiment thus provides a covert method for measuring negative reactions to minorities—covert in the strict sense of allowing us to measure negative reactions without respondents being aware we are measuring them. No technique is perfect, very much including the list experiment. But we are not aware of a better one in public opinion research for covert measurement.

The heart of the matter is whether those who have strongly negative views of how Muslims treat women and children—but positive ones of Muslims in general—are presenting themselves as more tolerant and egalitarian than they truly are. What should be true if they

---

[23] In selecting the items on the list, a vital consideration was to avoid a "ceiling" effect. Suppose you compose a list of items that very often make people angry. Say, on average, people get angry or upset at three of the four items. If, on average, people get angry at three of the four items, that means that in the baseline condition a substantial proportion get angry at all four. And that means, in turn, that in the treatment condition their counterparts who additionally are angry at minorities would, if they were to answer truthfully, answer five. But since there are only five items on the list, to give the answer five is of course to express anger at minorities openly—which defeats the whole purpose of the list experiment. Accordingly, a primary purpose of pretesting was to ensure that the average number of angry responses to the list in the baseline condition was less than two, ensuring that scarcely a handful would ever pick four. We would also observe that the test item is inserted in the middle of the list, rather than at the head of the list or asked at the end in order to avoid either a recency or primacy effect.

in fact dislike Muslims but do not wish to say so openly? Since there is no need in the list experiment to simulate a socially acceptable appearance, they should take advantage of the opportunity to express opposition to ethnic minorities when they are given a chance to do so.

Let us call those who say they take exception to Muslim treatment of women and children—but do not take exception to Muslims themselves—"liberal critics." The label means nothing by itself: precisely what is at issue is whether "liberal critics" are liberal.

Table 2.5 shows the mean number of angry responses in the baseline and test conditions, and the percentage difference between them (together with standard errors) for every relevant group. The reactions of the large segment of Dutch society we have called liberal critics in the baseline and the test conditions are statistically indistinguishable. They do not take advantage of the opportunity to react negatively to minorities even when they believe no one could observe them doing so. By contrast, approximately a third of that small segment of Dutch society that has a positive attitude toward Muslims in every respect appear to react negatively. It is tempting to view their reaction as revealing the genuine views of the politically correct; possibly also correct, but the standard error is very large, and the finding only barely meets conventional levels of significance. And we can see that the list experiment does identify those who do dislike minorities. A very large number of those who dislike Muslims in general—slightly more than half, in fact—take advantage of the apparent cloak of privacy

TABLE 2.5
Covert Measures of Prejudice: The List Experiment

"Pure" liberals (N = 70)			"Critical" liberals (N = 217)			Anti-Muslims (N = 284)		
Baseline	Test	Percent angry	Baseline	Test	Percent angry	Baseline	Test	Percent angry
1.19	1.57	38	1.56	1.66	11	1.64	2.18	54
(.13)	(1.62)	(21)	(.11)	(.1)	(15)	(.05)	(.1)	(13)

to object to assistance for minorities. In short, the list experiment works as it should. It picks out those who do dislike minorities. All in all, the results of the list experiment indicate that those who say that they object to Muslim practices—but not to Muslims—mean what they say.

Here we reach the limits of the evidence. Our results go against the claim that Dutch who object only to Muslim treatment of women and children are secretly hiding a dislike of Muslims or minorities in general. Our results instead are consistent with a conclusion that they are registering their objections based on principle.[24] We recognize that some will not accept this conclusion. They take the position that to object to the practice of one culture from the perspective of another is, in and of itself, ethnocentrism. This of course is a normative argument, not an empirical one and, in this particular context, not a coherent one. What could it mean to argue that, in a liberal culture like the Netherlands, it is ethnocentric to invoke liberal values as a normative standard?[25] But it is not necessary for an argument to be valid in order for it to be believed.

VALUE CONFLICT AND VALUE PLURALISM

The Dutch object to Muslim treatment of women and children; Muslim immigrants object to the Dutch treatment of women and children. In both cases, to say that what the other group does is not right, is to raise the question of their right to do it. But the Dutch are in a position to do something about their objections in a way that Muslim immigrants are not. A conflict of values aggravates group conflict: it increases opposition to "the other" living in their lives in the light of not merely different but opposing values.

This seemed an obvious truth to us; so much so that it did not occur to us until near the end of this project to test whether it is true. The

---

[24] We have presented here our two most-on-point findings. We have performed many other tests. All the results are consistent with those presented here.

[25] For the different, and difficult, question of how liberal values apply to illiberal societies, see Hollis 2002.

results of our covert measure of prejudice indicate that the large part of the Dutch public that objects to Muslim treatment of women and children—but not to Muslims—is tolerant. If those results are valid, what else might they believe?

They might believe that Muslims have a right to follow their own way of life in the Netherlands. "Might" deserves to be underlined. Many Dutch believe—indeed, believe strongly—that certain Muslim practices are wrong and that the values that underlie them are not merely different from, but opposed to, Western European values. It would be understandable—whether justifiable or not—if they believe that Muslims who have chosen to come to live in their country must conform to the way of life of their new country. On the other hand, if these Dutch are, indeed, tolerant as our findings indicate, and if tolerance involves a positive regard for minorities as we have suggested, they may be prepared to go further than merely "putting up" with Muslims. They may take the position that Muslims have a right to live their lives as they wish, notwithstanding the fact that certain aspects of the way they live collide with the values of Dutch society. This would not, of course, be an unlimited right. But within broad and admittedly vague limits—broad because vague—the principle is that other people should be able to live their lives the way they believe they ought to be lived.

We have two ways to test this conjecture, one negative, the other positive. The negative test is whether people in the majority require that minorities conform to the values of the majority culture. We asked whether Turks and Moroccans—that is, Muslim immigrants— "should have to adapt to the Dutch way of life."[26]

The vertical axis of figure 2.2 indicates the probability of requiring assimilation: the higher the plotted line, the higher the likelihood of requiring assimilation. Again the level of overall hostility to Muslims is plotted along the horizontal line; the dotted line describes the reactions of those most critical of Muslim treatment of women and children; the solid line the reactions of those most favorable to it. And

[26] The specific wording is: "Most Turks and Moroccans have freely come to the Netherlands, and therefore should have to adapt to the Dutch way of life."

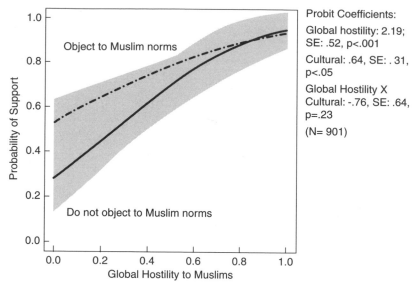

Fig. 2.2. Support for assimilation

again the shaded areas describe the confidence intervals around the estimates. As you can see, the probability that those who have positive attitudes in every respect will believe that Muslims should assimilate is strikingly low: there is only about a 25 percent chance they will do so. It is all the more striking, then, that the reactions of those who object to Muslim treatment of women and children—but not to Muslims—are identical.[27]

Declining to require that minorities conform to the larger society's way of life is not a small thing. But it is far from everything. It is a large step further to affirmatively declare that they have a right to live as they believe they should, even though it means regularly doing what the larger society believes is wrong. We accordingly asked whether minorities—Muslim minorities in particular—"have the right to follow their own way of life."[28] Figure 2.3 plots the probabil-

[27] That is, are statistically indistinguishable.

[28] The specific wording is: "Since the Netherlands is a free country, Turks and Moroccans who have come here have the right to follow their own way of life."

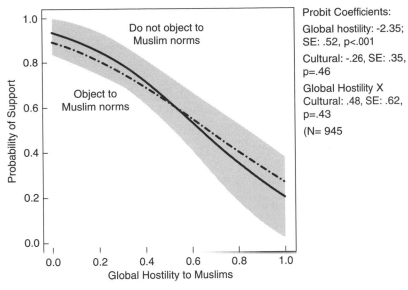

Probit Coefficients:

Global hostility: -2.35;
SE: .52, p<.001

Cultural: -.26, SE: .35,
p=.46

Global Hostility X
Cultural: .48, SE: .62,
p=.43

(N= 945

Fig. 2.3. Support for cultural pluralism

ity of support for the principle of cultural pluralism as a function of global hostility to Muslims and hostility to Muslim treatment of women and children.

Not surprisingly, support for cultural pluralism decreases sharply as global hostility to Muslims increases. Still, the small number of Dutch whose attitudes are positive toward Muslims in every respect are overwhelmingly supportive of the right of Muslim immigrants to follow their own way of life in the Netherlands. The odds are better than 90 percent that they will do so. That is impressive, but what is more impressive—indeed, took us quite by surprise—is the reaction of those who have a negative view of how Muslims treat women and children but a positive view of Muslims themselves. They are just as likely as those with a positive attitude toward Muslims in every respect to support cultural pluralism. The solid and the dotted lines statistically sit on top of each other: those who object to some Muslim practices but not to Muslims are just as overwhelmingly likely to support the right of Turks and Moroccans to follow their own ways of life as are those whose responses to Muslims are positive in every respect.

We appreciate that others, including many who have given much thought to the issue of diversity, will feel that this falls short. It is not enough to affirm the right of others to follow their own way of life. It is necessary to go further: necessary to use public funds to sustain the institutions—communal, religious, cultural—that sustain a minority's way of life; and necessary to use public authority to affirm that their way of life is as worth living as the larger society's way of life. Support for cultural pluralism, which is what we focus on, is not the same as support for multiculturalism, which is what they believe is required.[29]

True enough, the two are different. But as we see it, the willingness of those who reject certain Muslim values—but accept Muslims themselves—affirmatively to support the right of Muslim immigrants to follow their own way of life is itself an indication that supporters of multiculturalism have misunderstood the meaning of tolerance. On their view, it is a modest achievement. It requires only that people be willing to put up with those who differ in religious belief or ethnic identity. This gets things fundamentally wrong. Dutch who strongly take exception to Muslim treatment of women and children—who see in them a denial of the fundamental values of equality and respect for the individual—are not merely not insisting on assimilation; they are not merely ready to put up with them faute de mieux. They go farther. They take the position that Muslims in Western Europe have a *right* to follow their own way of life. Perhaps this is not far enough to satisfy many political theorists. It is, however, much farther than most students of liberal democracy had a right to expect.

AN ISSUE OF LOYALTY

The clash of Dutch and Muslim values does not lead the Dutch to reject Muslims precisely because the values of Dutch society are liberal values. But the combination of value conflict and multiculturalism does exact a cost. Raising the barriers to immigration is part of it but by no means the largest part of it. One specific negative evaluation is

---

[29] See Verkuyten 2005b.

made far more frequently than for Muslims. They are twice as likely as other minorities to be judged "politically untrustworthy"—about four out of ten Dutch say so, which is not all that far from an absolute majority of the general public. Figure 2.4 plots the probability of characterizing Muslim immigrants as "politically untrustworthy" on the vertical axis: the higher the line, the more probable the character- ization. The degree to which respondents dislike Muslims pure and simple is plotted along the horizontal axis: the further to the right, the greater the dislike. And again the dotted line describes the reactions of those most opposed to Muslim treatment of women and children, the solid line those who are most favorable.

The higher the level of overall hostility to Muslims, the higher the probability that respondents perceive Muslims to be politically un- trustworthy—no surprise here. Now, look at those who are the most positive in their overall attitudes toward Muslims—those at the far left of the figure 2.4. If they do not take exception to Muslim treat- ment of women and children, the odds are only about one out of ten that they will say Muslims are politically untrustworthy; if they do

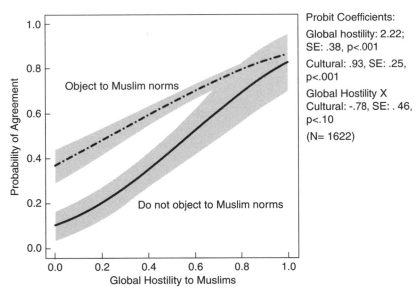

Fig. 2.4. "Muslim immigrants are politically untrustworthy"

take exception, the odds are in the neighborhood of four out of ten that they will perceive them as politically untrustworthy. Conflicts of values matter for supporters of liberal values, this suggests, because they can signify divided loyalties.

There is no logical necessity at work here, we want to emphasize. Conflicts of values can be accommodated in liberal societies; indeed, they can be accommodated far more readily, our results indicate, than has been recognized. But a policy that insists on fundamental differences between majority and minority can give them a meaning that no one intended.

"Politically untrustworthy" carries the implication of a fifth column—a group within the society secretly at war with it or prepared to war against it. It would be one thing if this charge of disloyalty were confined to the margins of society, to the prejudiced and closed-minded who in any case want to criticize and demean Muslim minorities. But it is not. "Politically untrustworthy" is the inference drawn by the very people who support the right of Muslim minorities to live their own way of life even in face of a conflict of values. The liberal center, not just the illiberal periphery, believe Muslim minorities still give their deepest loyalty to the country they came from. They have come to profit from their new country, not to become a part of it.

The focus of multiculturalism has been on the importance of—in a word of our times—privileging differences between majority and minority cultures. It has not been on the importance of giving one's loyalty to the larger society, still less of demonstrating it. Rather, it has been the reverse. The issue of allegiance, of committing oneself to one's new country and its institutions, has been seen as either unnecessary or in conflict with the principles of multiculturalism. The result has been a widespread belief that Muslim minorities still give their loyalty to the country and culture they came from, not the one they now live in.

It is in equal measure remarkable and regrettable that a suspicion of disloyalty was widespread before the tragic parade of events—September 11; Moroccans' cheering the collapse of the World Trade Center shown on Dutch television; and the burning of mosques and churches in the wake of the ritual slaying of Theo van Gogh.

CHAPTER 3

Prejudice

IT SOMETIMES IS DIFFICULT to understand what people mean when they talk about a minority group. But often it is all too obvious. Listen to the words of Rob, from Rotterdam: "That Moroccan family next door was back home again, they steal bikes like a magpie, they bring their friends in for it and last week or so I think, what is that noise, who is hammering, and I look outside, and there sits this monkey, this little Moroccan, sits there with a bike lock that is rusted and puts de-rusting oil on it, and is hammering on it."[1] The characterization is stinging—Moroccans "steal bikes like a magpie." It is "they"—not an individual, not a particular family, but Moroccans in general ("they bring their friends in for it") who are criminal. The tone is striking—"there sits this monkey, this little Moroccan." To say that he dislikes Moroccans does not come close to capturing his feelings. He is angry, and not at his or their circumstances but at them. He has disdain for them, and—we stress—feels quite comfortable publicly, explicitly expressing his hostility and contempt.

Hostility, contempt, and aversion are marks of prejudice. We do not want to give an impression that they need be this intense to qualify as prejudice; still less that they always are this transparent. But feelings as intense as these are expressed far more commonly than is recognized. Listen to Jan, also a resident of Rotterdam, also speaking in a group: "[They] are ashamed of their own kind, those that come from the gutter. And they don't give a shit about anything, children walk on the street till eleven at night, uh, you name it, sandwich in

[1] Verkuyten 1997, 117.

their hands and out on the street again. There is no order and regularity in their household."[2] Read those words again. We need to use numbers to convey the magnitude of the problem. But the feelings that underlie them—the hostility and contempt for minorities—need always to be remembered.[3]

Prejudice's power partly comes from its ability to propel people to action; partly from its capacity to coordinate an image of the "other." Individuals who make up the "other" recede as individuals; what remains is an image of a group. Some members of the group still stand out, but more often than not it is precisely because they are the "exception" that proves the rule. Seeing another as the "other" minimizes awareness of differences among them and maximizes perceptions of difference between "them" and "us."[4] It could be said that social intolerance—we use the words "prejudice" and "intolerance" synonymously—is grounded in the negative evaluation of difference. It would be closer to the mark to observe that difference in and of itself is a ground for negative evaluation.[5]

Some social categories imply difference by default. The term for immigrants in the Netherlands, for example, is *allochtons* (those from another soil). Not surprisingly, they are viewed as dark, foreign, intrusive, working class, and deviant. Difference and deviance are the constituent elements of the "other."[6] Distrust naturally follows. "They" will take what is "ours," without making reciprocal contributions as they should; or following rules of proper and legal behavior as they should; or exercising restraint and self-control to the extent that they should. Avoidance and fear is the response, empathy is switched off, and the focus is on self-protection.[7]

---

[2] Ibid., 70.

[3] Curiously, there are endless conceptual definitions of prejudice. For a relatively recent and theoretically nonpartisan overview, see Duckitt 2001; for the classic synthesis, see Allport 1988.

[4] Brown 1986; McCauley and Stitt 1978; McCauley, Stitt, and Segal 1980.

[5] See the classic work of Tajfel (1982), who called attention to the pivotal role of mere categorization.

[6] Hagendoorn and Hraba 1989; Hagendoorn and Kleinpenning 1991.

[7] Social attitudes, such as social conformity and tough-mindedness, may reinforce these

The classic definition of prejudice is Allport's: "antipathy based on a faulty and inflexible generalization."[8] But two of the three elements are famously elusive. What, for example, is the difference between being inflexible and being staunch in holding to a belief? How could one tell in a public opinion interview that a person was one rather than the other? And what is a "faulty . . . generalization"? Is it a characterization that, though true of some members of a group, is false for most? We shall see that there is a stereotype of Moroccan immigrants as criminal. In what sense is this "stereotype" false? Not all Moroccan immigrants are criminal; not even most. But social statistics back up the common image of them as criminal. Second- as well as first-generation Moroccans face criminal charges more often than does the Dutch population or do other immigrant groups.[9] More commonly, objective benchmarks are not available. Then it is still more difficult to determine what is real and what is exaggerated. Few social scientists have been willing to tackle the task of distinguishing between attributed and actual characteristics of minorities.[10] But if the boundaries of prejudice are fuzzy, how can we know that prejudice is there when it is there and that it is not there when it is not? Hostility is the key.[11] Indiscriminately ascribing negative characteristics to minorities—describing them as lazy, untrustworthy, selfish, and the like—is an expression of antipathy. Hence our definition of prejudice: a readiness to belittle minorities, to dislike them, to shun them, to be contemptuous of them, and to feel hostility toward them—"there sits this monkey, this little Moroccan."[12]

The number and variety of minorities in the Netherlands are im-

---

reactions because they are based on general beliefs in a threatening world or a competitive society (see Duckitt 2001 for an overview).

[8] Allport 1988, 9.

[9] Jaarrapport Integratie SCP 2005, 148–49.

[10] Only a comparison of the *actual* traits of immigrant groups with the traits *attributed* to them makes clear what is exaggerated and what is not. Therefore Bogardus (1950) proposed to compare *stereotypes* with *sociotypes*. Sociotypes reflect the actual characteristics of groups. This ingenious solution is not easily applicable in research.

[11] For a different view, see Dovidio, Glick, and Rudman 2005.

[12] Sniderman et al. 2000, 24.

portant to appreciate. By a small margin, Surinamese make up the largest group and are ethnically diverse, comprising former slaves from Africa, Indian Hindus from India, and creoles from Latin America.[13] Their ethnic diversity notwithstanding, they share a great advantage. Surinam was a Dutch colony; unlike other immigrant minorities, Surinamese immigrants therefore speak Dutch fluently, indeed, were socialized in Dutch culture. The largest number of them—almost half of the population of Surinam—came to the Netherlands in the 1970s when Surinam became an independent state, and they are on average more educated and less often unemployed than other migrant groups in the Netherlands. Asylum seekers and political refugees have come from many countries and regions—Iran, Iraq, Somalia, Latin America, Sri Lanka—none with a linguistic or cultural connection to the Netherlands. When the Netherlands needed cheap labor in the 1960s and 1970s, low-skilled "guest workers" were imported in large numbers from the Middle East (mainly Turkey) and Northern Africa (mainly Morocco). The Turkish immigrants predominantly came from rural areas in eastern Turkey and, not surprisingly, were highly traditional in their ways and beliefs. Moroccan immigrants were also traditional in their values. The distinctive characteristic of Turkish and Moroccan migrants is that they are Muslims and distance themselves from the strong secular trends in Dutch society.

Although all the groups lag behind the Dutch in educational level, Dutch-language proficiency, and employment,[14] there are significant differences among them. Surinamese are better-off in terms of educational achievement, employment, and occupational achievement; Turks and Moroccans are less well-off on all three counts.[15] More discouraging, the second and third generation of immigrants are not doing markedly better than the first did. Many had come with their mothers to join fathers who had been sending money every month to feed them. These youngsters had grown up without their fathers and were more unruly than was the tradition in Turkey and Morocco.

---

[13] Hagendoorn, Veenman, and Vollebergh 2003b.

[14] Van Amersfoort 1974; Penninx 1988.

[15] Hagendoorn, Veenman, and Vollebergh 2003b.

After they arrived in the Netherlands, most of them did not do well in school and could not find jobs. Many ended up at loose ends, trading drugs and committing petty crime. Young Moroccan males in particular became notorious for engaging in street crime, stealing, robbing, and pickpocketing in Rotterdam and Amsterdam in the late 1990s.

To measure prejudice toward each of the immigrant minorities, we went through a list of attributes and asked, one by one, if they applied to most members of specific minorities.[16] For instance, the interviewer asks, "Do you agree or disagree that most [group X] are selfish—that is, they think only about themselves, without concern about others?" The question no doubt is too simpleminded for some respondents and too negative for others, but either way, they can simply decline to answer.[17] If they do answer, they can give one of four possible answers: strongly disagree, disagree somewhat, agree somewhat, or strongly agree. In all, they are asked about eight possible characterizations of minorities—as honest, selfish, slackers, intrusive, law-abiding, complainers, violent, and inferior. The list includes two characteristics that are positive to avoid tapping a bias toward negative answers regardless of the actual content of the question. To be classified as prejudiced, a respondent will have to give positive answers to negatively phrased questions and negative answers to positively phrased questions.

We went through the list of eight twice in order to obtain people's views about four groups of immigrant minorities. On the first pass, people were asked either about Turkish or Moroccan immigrants; on the second, either about Surinamese or asylum seekers. Who was asked about whom was, of course, decided on a purely random basis—a property we shall exploit. The four minority groups, as we noted, have different places of origin, languages, historical experiences, and levels of familiarity with Western European culture and of human capital (as indexed, for example, by education) and hence different levels of diffi-

[16] For evidence of validity of this measure of prejudice, see Sniderman et al. 2000.

[17] It should be stressed that respondents not only were free to refuse to be interviewed but also were instructed that they were free to decline to answer any question they did not wish to answer. This option of "exit" makes all the more relevant our *covert* measure of negative affect. See chapter 5.

culty in fitting into a Western European society and economy. To the degree that they in fact differ, they should evoke different reactions.

Figure 3.1 shows that some points of difference are detectable. Moroccans are more likely than other minorities to be characterized as dishonest, violent, intrusive, and not law-abiding—all, as it were, aspects of a criminal image. It should be noted that Moroccans, not Muslims per se, have this criminal image: Turkish immigrants are perceived in more or less the same hue as refugees and Surinamese.

The dominant pattern of evaluative judgments, though, is one of similarity, not dissimilarity. Consider judgments of whether minorities are trustworthy. One would assume that social relations require trust, otherwise people will tend to avoid one another. Do the Dutch respondents trust immigrants? In the neighborhood of 30 percent say that the three of the groups, Turks, refugees, and Surinamese, are not honest, with a larger number, 40 percent, saying the same about Moroccans. Take another negative characteristic: violent. When people think that there is a fair chance that a member of one of the immigrant groups cannot be trusted, this lack of trust can rather easily be acted out by avoiding contact and transactions with members of this group. Not so with violence. Violence is harder to protect against, so the social environment is more threatening. It accordingly is worth remarking that around 30 percent think that Turks, refugees, and Surinamese are violent, again with a larger number, 40 percent, thinking the same of Moroccans. The numbers endorsing another element of an image of criminality are still higher. On the order of 40 percent *deny* that immigrant minorities are law-abiding—deny, that is, that "they behave like good citizens, observing the regulations and laws of the state." In sum, on the order of a third of the Dutch population view immigrant groups as criminal, dishonest, and violent—a negative image to say the least. Nor is the image of criminality the only negative element of the image of immigrant minorities. Never less than a quarter of the Dutch population say that immigrant minorities try to avoid working; behave in an annoying and insistent way; think only about themselves; and try to make others feel sorry for them. In addition, almost one out of ten Dutch evaluates each of the four immigrant groups as inferior.

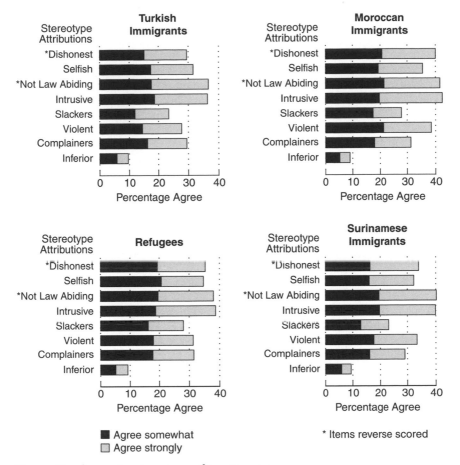

Fig. 3.1. Dutch negative stereotypes of immigrant groups

It has become a cliché that people will not express derogatory views of minority groups—at any rate publicly—for fear of being labeled racist. So far as we can tell, this cliché owes its plausibility to the force of repetition. It is certainly not sustained by the weight of evidence, as these results make plain.[18]

[18] A conclusion of Bobo 2001, 14, summarizing the discussion of a focus group on race in America, is apt: "In an era when everyone supposedly knows what to say and what not to say and is artful about avoiding overt bigotry, this group discussion still quickly turned to racial topics and quickly elicited unabashed negative stereotyping and antiblack hostility." See also Sniderman and Piazza 1993.

A LITANY OF COMPLAINTS

Prejudice is a litany of complaints about "them;" it has the typical structure of complaining: they have this annoying or vexing characteristic, and that one, and so on. One negative remark brings to mind another. The unifying theme is dislike, hostility, even contempt, and the evaluation tends to be indiscriminate, lumping different minorities together, because even if they differ in some respects, "they" are all part of the larger immigrant "them."

Do specific criticisms of minorities constitute a litany of complaints? The answer to the question is not difficult to find. If there are different underlying themes in the negative evaluations, then a factor analysis should produce the different factors to which they correspond. (It does so by testing for the similarity of the underlying response and by tracing a principal component in their correlations.) To the degree that each complaint runs into another, and the specifics of each are relatively unimportant, a factor analysis will uncover one dominant factor.

Figure 3.2 presents the results of a factor analysis visually to make the results immediately intelligible.[19] The height of the columns indicates the size of a dimension, its eigenvalue. For a factor to be considered substantively significant, its eigenvalue must be greater than one.[20] A less mechanical approach is to find the place in each plot where the smooth decrease in eigenvalues appears to level off. The effective number of dimensions is the number of eigenvalues to the left of that point.[21] In either case, the conclusion is the same. For each outgroup's scree plot, the "elbow" appears at the second eigenvalue. For all minority groups, then, there is only one factor with an eigenvalue larger than 1, and it captures the degree to which people consistently evaluate minorities negatively or positively.

In reality, of course, the four minority groups—refugees and asylum seekers, Turkish immigrants, Surinamese, and Moroccan immi-

---

[19] We are indebted to John Bullock for the analysis that follows.

[20] This is the oft-used Kaiser (1960) criterion. The rationale is simple: dimensions with eigenvalues smaller than 1 have less explanatory power than one of the original variables.

[21] Cattell 1966.

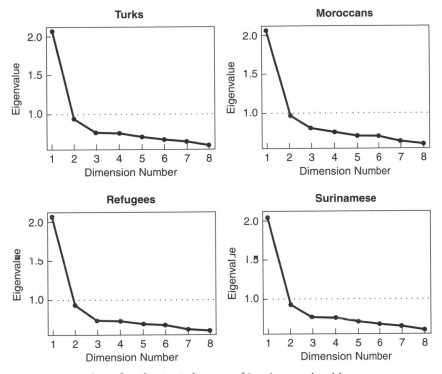

Fig. 3.2. Scree plots of evaluative judgments of immigrant minorities

grants—differ in a great number of ways—cultural, religious, and national. The fact that each taps the same common dimension is therefore all the more striking. But here is a more demanding test: Does each negative stereotype distinguish *with the same degree of efficiency* between the most and least prejudiced toward each of the four minority groups?

Think about mathematical aptitude. Ideally, a test of it would consist of questions that have a high degree of power in discriminating the mathematically adept from the mathematically inept. So, too, with a test of prejudice. Some questions have more power, others less, to discriminate between those who are more and those who are less prejudiced. The technology for estimating the power of items to discriminate is based on Item Response Theory (IRT), a workhorse tool in

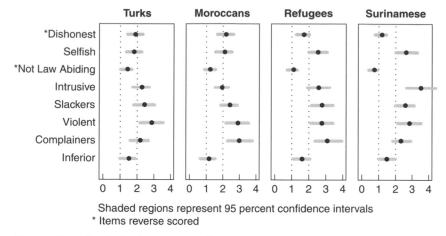

Fig. 3.3. Item discrimination estimates for immigrant groups

educational testing.[22] The four columns of figure 3.3 report results for each of the four groups;[23] plotted points indicate item discrimination estimates; and thick grey bars represent 95 percent confidence intervals. All items to the right of the left vertical line within each column have discrimination estimates greater than 1.0, a conventional standard for good discrimination. All items to the right of the right line have discrimination estimates greater than 2.0, which means they discriminate extremely well.[24]

As an example, look at the first column, which presents evaluative judgments of Turkish immigrants. Two of the negative evaluations do less well than the other six: (not) "law-abiding" and "inferior by nature." They have the least discriminatory power for two of the other groups, Moroccans and refugees, and nearly so for the fourth, Surinamese. There is some appearance of variation from group to group. "Violent" has the most power for Turks; "violent" and "complainers" for Moroccans; "complainers" for refugees; and "intrusive"

[22] Hambleton, Swaminathan, and Rogers 1991. For a nontechnical introduction to IRT, see Henard 2004.

[23] Rejecting a positive characterization of a minority group is treated as equivalent to accepting a negative one.

[24] Hambleton, Swaminathan, and Rogers 1991.

for Surinamese. But for practical purposes, when one takes into account the margin of error, the remaining six items have essentially the same power to discriminate between more and less prejudiced for all four minority groups. The results of the item discrimination analysis thus complement the results of the factor analysis. Together, they justify combining responses to six of the eight evaluations. We call the combined measure the stereotype index. Consistency—across criticisms and across groups—is the hallmark of prejudice.

LEVELS OF PREJUDICE: THE NETHERLANDS AND ITALY

Prejudice, we have said, expresses itself in a systematic, indiscriminate readiness to dislike members of another group by virtue of their membership in the group. How many of our respondents run through the full litany of complaints? How many make none? Table 3.1 shows the percentages of respondents agreeing with one or more of the six negative characteristics of each group. The first feature that stands out is the mean. There is some variation between groups. Surinamese have the least negative image ($x = 1.4$); Moroccans the most ($x = 1.9$). Still, the average for all four groups is less than 2.

At first glance it appears encouraging to observe that the average number of negative attributions is so low; that never less than a third and once nearer a half make no negative evaluations at all; and that, setting Moroccans outside, a good majority, never less than 60 percent, make at most one. A closer look is less reassuring. Our respondents had six opportunities to say something negative about a minority. There is no magic cut point, but for the sake of argument, consider how many of them took advantage of at least half or more of them. The number varies slightly depending on the minority. But it is never less than a quarter of the population and in the case of Moroccans as much as a third.

These are not small numbers by any standard. But it is not merely a matter of how many will agree with many negative evaluations of minorities. It also is a question of how many will agree with the most offensive characterizations. Consider people who took at least half of

TABLE 3.1
Number of Negative Evaluations of Immigrant Groups

Number of negative evaluations	Turks (%)	Moroccans (%)	Asylum seekers and refugees (%)	Surinamese (%)
0	39	34	40	46
1	21	18	21	19
2	13	14	12	11
3	9	12	10	8
4	8	10	7	6
5	6	8	6	6
6	5	5	4	4
Mean	1.6	1.9	1.6	1.4
Sample size	980	955	981	937

the opportunities they had to voice negative evaluations of minorities as prejudiced. What are they saying? Are these minor criticisms? Or are they saying the nastiest things possible? The answer is the nastiest possible. Never less than three out of every four, and sometimes four out of every five—depending on the minority group they are evaluating—characterize minorities as violent.

Common folklore has it that the Dutch like complaining, and common sense has it that the most common way of starting a conversation is by complaining about the weather. Complaining may be part of a cultural habit. On the other hand, the Dutch have a reputation for tolerance. Is this reputation deserved?

In an earlier study, we investigated prejudice in Italy.[25] The measures in the two studies are exactly the same, as is the method of interviewing. Naturally, the minorities who are the victims of prejudice

[25] Sniderman et al. 2000; see especially chapter 2.

are not. In the Dutch study there are four: Moroccans, Turks, Surinamese, and asylum seekers. In the Italian study there were three: North Africans, Central Africans, and Eastern Europeans. Table 3.2 shows the numbers of negative characterizations made by Italians for each of the three groups.

If you are Dutch, there is good news and bad. On the one side, twice as many Dutch as Italians make no negative characterizations of minorities. On the other side, roughly equivalent numbers in both countries make three or more. The Dutch by this criterion are as intolerant as Italians. One might reasonably argue that the circumstances were different. The Italian figures were obtained near the middle of the 1990s; the Dutch toward the end of the 1990s. The problems of immigrant minorities in general had become more severe, and this

TABLE 3.2

Number of Negative Evaluations of Immigrant Groups: Italy vs. the Netherlands

Number of negative characterizations	Italian responses			Dutch responses			
	North Africans (%)	Central Africans (%)	Eastern Europeans (%)	Turks (%)	Moroccans (%)	Asylum seekers and refugees (%)	Surinamese (%)
0	19	22	23	39	34	40	46
1	20	25	22	21	18	21	19
2	23	20	18	13	14	12	11
3	16	12	14	9	12	10	8
4	10	11	10	8	10	7	6
5	9	8	8	6	8	6	6
6	3	2	3	5	5	4	4
Mean	2.2	2	2	1.6	1.9	1.6	1.4
Sample size	504	456	920	980	955	981	937

was particularly true of Muslim immigrants—the focus of the Dutch study. Either or both are plausible reasons to expect that the level of intolerance in Italy would have been higher if the two studies had been done at the same time—plausible but no more. Based on the evidence at hand, two things appear to be true: first, the proportion of tolerant people is higher in the Netherlands than in Italy; and second, the proportion of intolerant people is approximately the same in the two countries.

The Indiscriminateness of Prejudice

It is an affectation of the intolerant that they make distinctions—they cannot abide one minority group but accept another. Here is an exchange among three people—Gerda, Bram, and Truus.

GERDA: What you see there is that it is often Moroccan youth who are doing it.
BRAM: Yes, in that bar they are almost always Moroccans.
TRUUS: Yea, but Moroccans is really bad, isn't it?
GERDA: That is what you really see.
TRUUS: Because Turkish people are by the way not so bad as Moroccans.
GERDA: Yea, in that bar.
TRUUS: Because they are really trash, gosh, really trash.[26]

The hostility and contempt that are trademarks of prejudice are explicit: Moroccans are "really trash, gosh, really trash." But, so, too, is a claim to making distinctions between minorities: "Turkish people are by the way not so bad as Moroccans." We mean to show that this is a distinction without a difference. Prejudice is blind in a deep sense. It reflects a dislike not of a particular minority but of minorities in general.

A thought experiment will convey what we have in mind. Imagine a small knot of Dutch on a street corner late one night. They are talk-

---

[26] Verkuyten 1997, 70.

ing about Turkish immigrants, some expressing unalloyed criticism, others disagreeing. Down the street is another group of Dutch. They, too, are talking about Turkish immigrants, some complaining, others not. But then, after fifteen minutes or so, this second group switches the topic of conversation. Instead of continuing to debate the qualities of Turkish immigrants, they start talking about asylum seekers. Imagine also that you were on the same block, midway between the two groups of Dutch, close enough to both to be able to make out the tenor of the two conversations, but far enough away to be unable to hear precisely *who* the subject of discussion in either conversation was. Imagining all of this, our thought experiment turns on one question. Could you tell that, partway through their conversation, the second group had switched which immigrants they were talking about while the first had not?

To carry out our thought experiment, we need at least two minorities and two measures of prejudice toward each. The stereotype measure supplies one; Bogardus's classic measure of social distance, the second.[27] Specifically, we asked how attractive respondents would find having an immigrant minority as a neighbor and a life partner. Our focus is thus intimate contact. Neighbors meet frequently and unintentionally. They may need each other for practical assistance and if they have children of the same age, the children may want to play together. If one lives in an apartment, the consequences may be even more direct and consequential: neighbors may be loud and they may be intrusive; and partnership and marriage anchor the pole of intimate contact. Of course, a person might dislike the idea of having a member of an immigrant minority as a neighbor not out of prejudice but as the result of an unhappy experience. But again our interest is not in idiosyncratic judgments but in consistent, systematic, negative reactions to minorities.

The test of our thought experiment is whether one can tell the difference between when respondents are reacting to the same group and when they are reacting to different groups. Table 3.3 reports the correlations between the negative stereotype measures and the social

---

[27] Bogardus 1925.

TABLE 3.3

The Switch Experiment: Correlations of Two Separate Measures of Prejudice for the Same Group and for Two Different Groups

	Turks	Moroccans	Refugees	Surinamese
Turks	0.57 (.02)	0.45 (.03)	0.45 (.03)	0.54 (.03)
Moroccans	0.50 (.03)	0.50 (.03)	0.46 (.03)	0.49 (.03)
Refugees	0.45 (.03)	0.46 (.03)	0.49 (.03)	0.48 (.03)
Surinamese	0.44 (.03)	0.35 (.03)	0.40 (.03)	0.53 (.03)

Diagonal median = .52, with standard error = .03; off-diagonal median = .46, with standard error = .03

distance measures. The numbers in the main diagonal, shown in italics, report the correlations between the two measures for the same group. The median value is .52 (with a standard error of .03). The median value of all the correlations off the main diagonal report the correlations between the two measures for different groups. The median value is .47 (with a standard error of .03). The difference between the two is not statistically significant, still less substantively significant. In short, you cannot tell the difference between a discussion about one minority group and another in which the discussants switched, midway through, to talking about a quite different group.

This is not at all to say that every minority group carries the same burden. On the contrary, there is a hierarchy of acceptability.[28] Our study was not designed to investigate ethnic hierarchies; we have only a handful of indicators. Even so, our results disclose the same gradient of acceptability as previous studies, though of course less distinctly given the paucity of measures in our study. As table 3.4 shows, Suri-

---

[28] Hagendoorn 1993; Hagendoorn 1995; Hagendoorn and Hraba 1989.

TABLE 3.4
Social Distance Measures

	Acceptance as neighbors (%)	Acceptance as partner (%)
Moroccans	68	39
Germans*	69	—
Refugees	70	38
Turks	73	40
Surinamese	81	53
Spaniards	87	60

*Only acceptance as neighbors question was asked about Germans.

namese, who speak Dutch and know Dutch culture, are more readily accepted as neighbors than Turks, refugees, and Moroccans, although the differences between the last three are small. Spaniards, however, are more readily accepted as neighbors than Surinamese. Germans, by contrast, are no more popular than Muslim immigrants and distinctly less popular than Surinamese—hardly surprisingly considering the German occupation of the Netherlands in World War II. Again not surprisingly, there is much more reluctance to accept minorities as life partners than neighbors; reassuringly, the basic hierarchy of minorities is the same. Surinamese are more readily accepted as partners than Turks, Moroccans, or refugees. Western Europeans, in the form of Spaniards, are more readily accepted than Surinamese.

Two things are clear, then. First, some minorities are ranked more highly than others. Second, those who are systematically hostile to one minority are as systematically hostile to others—also a key result for our purposes. It is precisely the readiness to dislike minorities that gives prejudice the power to drive the positions that people take on public policies dealing with minorities.

Rising Anger and Closing the Ranks

Our concern is politics. Prejudice reflects hostility; it also reflects anxiety. The connection between the two is natural: we tend to dislike those we find threatening, and we tend to find threatening those we dislike. Either way, the first line of defense politically is the policy at the border: immigration should be made more difficult, if it is not possible to make it impossible.

Figure 3.4 plots the probability of support for making immigration more difficult as a function of a person's overall level of prejudice. The probability of support for doing this is plotted on the vertical axis: the higher the line, the more probable opposition to continued immigration. The degree to which respondents are prejudiced is plotted along the horizontal axis: the further to the right, the greater the dislike. The shaded interval indicates the confidence intervals around the estimates.

Not surprisingly, the line rises from left to right. It would be astonishing if people who are prejudiced were not more likely to support stricter immigration than those who are tolerant. But what may

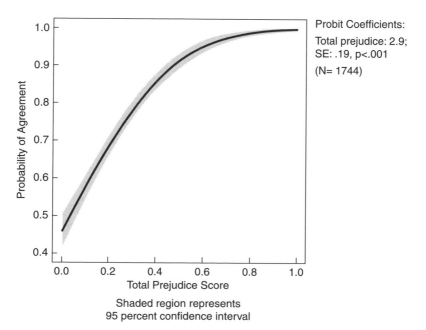

Probit Coefficients:
Total prejudice: 2.9;
SE: .19, p<.001
(N= 1744)

Shaded region represents
95 percent confidence interval

Fig. 3.4. "Immigration should be more difficult"

be surprising is the speed with which it shoots up. Even among the most tolerant, on the order of a half support raising the barriers to immigration, and the support for doing so rapidly becomes overwhelming. There is thus support for making immigration more difficult throughout the society.

Resistance to immigration is a line of defense for the intolerant but also for the tolerant—a sign of the depth of concern over immigrant minorities long before the violence that was to come. Some might respond that the breadth of resistance to immigration is a sign that the society as a whole is racist—not merely those who are overtly intolerant. It therefore is worth looking at reactions to the slogan "The Netherlands for the Dutch." This was the slogan of the Centrum Partij, a small racist party that emerged in the 1980s. The other Dutch political parties ignored the Centrum Partij, believing that paying no public attention to the issue of immigration was the best way to contain prejudice. The strategy was not without merit. The Centrum Partij soon collapsed due to internal struggle.

Figure 3.5 plots the probability of agreement with the slogan "The

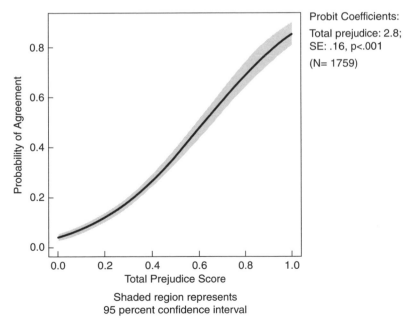

Fig. 3.5. "The Netherlands for the Dutch"

Netherlands for the Dutch" as a function of people's overall level of prejudice. All in all, a little under a third of our sample agree with the slogan—a substantial number by any reasonable standard; still more considering that the slogan had been expressly labeled racist. All the same, the trajectory of the curve in this figure differs sharply from the previous one. The probability of agreement starts off at a much lower level, rises steadily but gradually, passing fifty-fifty only among the more prejudiced.

The lesson we draw is that support for the first line of defense, checking immigration, is not confined to its intolerant segment. By contrast, substantial support for an openly racist society is concentrated in its most intolerant quarters.

THE OPEN REJECTION OF EQUALITY

Prejudice does have the power to propel people to support extremist policies. No doubt, one can quarrel whether particular policies are indeed extremist. But there is no doubt that an open rejection of equality for immigrant minorities qualifies as extremist. Curiously, though, the question of whether it is prejudice that is propelling people to support extremist policies is more difficult to answer than it may seem.

Obviously enough, bigots are more likely to reject equality for immigrant minorities than are tolerant people. But it does not follow they are doing so out of prejudice. Prejudice is just one current in a stream of aversive sentiments. Others, to cite the most obvious examples, are authoritarian and antidemocratic values. All three tend to go together: the most prejudiced are also the most committed to authoritarian and antidemocratic values.[29]

Is it prejudice that propels people to support policies that violate the values of a liberal democracy? As a theoretical matter, it is at least as plausible to take the position that opposition to democratic values is the primary factor, and prejudice appears to be a powerful force primarily because it is so strongly associated with antidemocratic values.

---

[29] The median intercorrelation of the three is .38.

The same holds true for authoritarian values. Prejudice may only appear to be a powerful factor because it is so strongly associated with authoritarianism. Accordingly, we take as the test of the power of prejudice to mold people's political positions the amount of influence it exerts *above and beyond* that of its companion aversive sentiments—authoritarian[30] and antidemocratic values.[31]

We have two pieces of evidence on the rejection of equality. The first is indirect—agreement with the statement: "Ethnic minorities now have *more rights* than they deserve."[32] Figure 3.6 lays out the results of three tests. The left-most panel plots the probability of agreement with this judgment depending on people's levels of prejudice—above and beyond their level of support for authoritarianism and antidemocratic values.[33] The middle panel plots the impact of support for authoritarian values—above and beyond their level of prejudice and antidemocratic values. The right-most panel plots the impact of support for antidemocratic values—above and beyond their level of prejudice and authoritarian values. We thus can get a clear picture of the difference each of the three makes independent of whatever difference that other two make.

Two findings stand out. First, each of the three factors significantly increases the probability of the agreement with the statement that "ethnic minorities now have more rights than they deserve" independently of the other two. Second, the impact of prejudice is mark-

---

[30] The measure of authoritarian values parallels the measure in the Italian study. It consists of summed responses to three items: "It is better to have a society with clear and strict rules than a society with too much freedom"; "Only the elderly, children, and disabled persons have the right to claim extra support from the state"; and "Whenever an employer finds it necessary to reduce the number of employees, the first to be laid off should be women with a husband with a paid job." The response format was modified (Likert: strongly or somewhat agree; strongly or somewhat disagree. Alpha = .53).

[31] The antidemocratic values index consists of summed responses to two statements: "We are better served by a strong leader than with democracy"; and "The interests of individuals should be subordinated to the interests of the people." The response format was modified (Likert; alpha = .47).

[32] Italics added for emphasis.

[33] Specifically, the values of the two other variables are set at their mean.

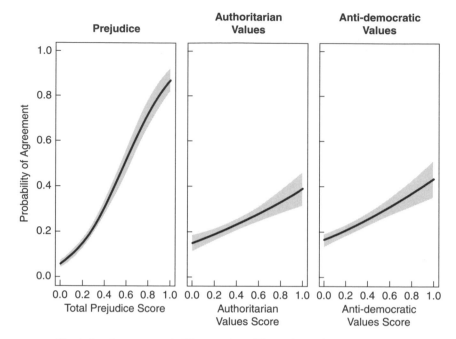

Shaded region represents 95 percent confidence interval

Probit Coefficients:
Total prejudice: 2.7; SE: .18, p<.001
Authoritarian values: .76, SE: .15, p<.001
Anti-democratic values: .81, SE: .14, p<.001
(N= 1695)

Fig. 3.6. "Minorities now have more rights than they deserve"

edly greater than that of authoritarian and antidemocratic values. As visual comparison of the three slopes shows, the estimated probability of agreement when the level of prejudice is set to its maximum is .87. By comparison, when authoritarian values and antidemocratic beliefs are set at their maximum, the estimated probability of agreement is .40 and .42, respectively.

One might reasonably ask, though, exactly what people have in mind when they say that minorities have more rights than they deserve. Are they really talking about "rights" at all? Possibly, the language of "rights" is being used metaphorically. The complaint is not that minorities literally have more legally enforceable claims but that they are getting more than their "fair share," say, of housing assistance or job-training programs. This may be unlikely to be correct; it is certainly ungenerous. But it is not (or, at any rate, not necessarily) a rejection of equal rights for minorities.

The heart of the matter is this: Are immigrant minorities entitled to equality in its most fundamental form—equality of rights? Accordingly, we asked, "Do you agree or disagree that ethnic minorities should have the same political and social rights as the Dutch people?" We take disagreement with this statement to be an open rejection of equality. Again the question is not whether the trio of factors we have focused on make it more likely that people will reject equality for immigrant minorities. Each does. The question instead is: How much of a difference does prejudice make—above and beyond the influence of authoritarian values and antidemocratic beliefs? So again we estimate the impact of each of the three, controlling for the other two.

The slopes of the curves in each of the three panels in figure 3.7 show that each of the factors significantly contributes to rejection of equal rights for minorities. There is a marked difference, though, in the steepness of the curves. When prejudice is at its maximum, the chances of rejecting equality for minorities are one out of two. By comparison, when authoritarian or antidemocratic values are at their maximum, the chances are more nearly one out of five.

It now is a common view in the psychological sciences—indeed, arguably the consensus view—that a concern about traditional forms of prejudice is out of date. Eagly and Dickman, for example, write that "many, if not most, of the important phenomena of everyday prejudice lie outside of the boundaries of [the traditional] framing of prejudice.[34] Jackman goes still further: "None of the intergroup relations (race, gender, or class) correspond to the expectations of [the traditional] prejudice model, i.e., free-ranging, hostile feelings or unmitigated, derogatory stereotypes."[35] Banaji, Nosek, and Greewald go further still. They contend that the belief that hostility toward victims

[34] Eagly and Dickman 2005, 29.
[35] Jackman 2005, 96.

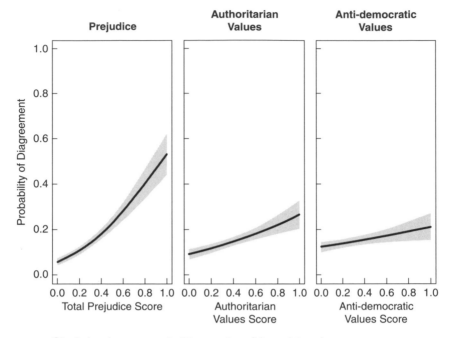

Shaded region represents 95 percent confidence interval

Probit Coefficients:
Total prejudice: 1.66; SE: .09, p<.001
Authoritarian values: .72, SE: .16, p<.001
Anti-democratic values: .36, SE: .14, p<.05
(N= 1688)

Fig. 3.7. "Minorities deserve equal rights"

of prejudice is the core of the contemporary problem of prejudice is scientifically out of date and, in a rebuke that we cannot get out of ears, that there is "no place for nostalgia in science."[36]

We can find no evidence consistent with any of these claims; all of it runs directly counter to all of them. Substantial numbers of the majority intensely dislike immigrant minorities. And there is not anything subtle about their feelings toward minorities or the positions they take

[36] Banaji, Nosek, and Greewald 2004.

based on them. Prejudice, our findings make plain, has the power to induce people to reject publicly the most fundamental form of equality for minorities—not equal outcomes or even equal opportunity, but equal rights.

PREJUDICE AND POLITICS

There is a political theory of intolerance. The political left assumed responsibility for issues of immigrant minorities. Mainstream parties of the left put in place policies to assist minorities in adapting to their new societies over a wide range of issues, including employment, education, policing, and the criminal justice system, even arts, media, and sports. It was natural for the left to do so, given its programmatic commitment to equality and presumption of government responsibility for social welfare. The mainstream right mainly acted with restraint, though when pressed by parties to their right they have fought back by bringing to the fore issues on which it held a natural advantage—crime, the importance of traditional values, and the need for stricter controls on immigration. Yet, restraint is the right word. A new politics was brought about by the eruption of extreme parties on the far right—Le Pen in France and Haider in Austria most conspicuously. These were figures beyond the pale. The basis of their support was a fusion of racism and right-wing extremism. The leadership of the mainstream right and left sometimes even set aside their competition and joined forces to enforce a cordon sanitaire. As long ago as 1968, in Great Britain, Heath, the leader of the Conservative Party, dismissed Powell from the party's shadow cabinet after his "Tiber River" speech. As recently as 2002, in France, the left supported the candidate of the right, Chirac, notwithstanding their disdain for him, to keep from power a candidate who was unthinkable, Le Pen. Fascism and anti-Semitism had gone together. Now racism and the extreme right go to together.

This is the pattern at the level of elite politics, and (it has seemed obvious to elites), it also is the pattern in the general public. Hence the identification of Fortuyn with LePen and the characterization of support for him as "not right wing but *extreme* right-wing."[37] Only the then prime minister, Wim Kok, saw that the problem went deeper. He used simple but apt metaphors. Prejudice, he said on one occasion, is a feeling "from the underbelly." On another, he warned that the "genie must remain in the bottle." The instructive feature of these metaphors is not what is said—the political virulence of prejudice— but what is not said—namely, the absence of the standard association of intolerance with the extreme political right. Prejudice, Kok was suggesting, can play a role across the political spectrum—even, possibly, as large a one on the left as on the right.

We take this to be an invitation to rethink the role of prejudice in politics. Our starting point is the conventional wisdom that the political right is less tolerant and more prejudiced than the political left. The conventional wisdom is not entirely wrong. There is an association between citizens' ideological orientation and their levels of prejudice: the further to the right they classify themselves, the more prejudiced they are likely to be. What is striking, though, is the modesty of the relationship between the two. In terms of a conventional correlation coefficient, the magnitude is only .24.[38] To get a sense of how small that is, the square of the coefficient is the amount of shared variance between the two—which is to say, 95 percent of the variation in prejudice and ideological orientation is separate. From a larger perspective, however, the conventional wisdom is right, but not for the reason conventionally given—that there is a close tie between political orientation and prejudice. It is right because there is a strong independent connection, quite apart from prejudice, between being on the political right and taking anti-immigrant political positions. For example, the correlation between ideological orientation and support for stricter immigration policies is .43, while the correlation between ideological orientation and support for the racist slogan "The Netherlands for the Dutch" is still higher—.52.

Our concern is the politics of prejudice, not those of ideology. Accordingly, we take as a starting point that people on the political right

---

[37] Van Holsteyn, Irwin, and den Ridder 2003, 71.

[38] Equivalent calculations for the American National Election Studies yield similar results.

have higher levels of prejudice than those on the left, although only modestly so, which is to say that there is no shortage of prejudice on the political left. The vital question, then, is what is the impact of prejudice on the political left?

No one supposes there is no prejudice on the left. But the conventional wisdom that the danger lies to the political right tacitly assumes that being on the left to some degree immunizes one against the effects of intolerance. If one stops and gives some thought to the matter, however, the assumption is not obviously plausible. What reason is there to suppose that the psychology of intolerance changes depending on the political perspective from which a person views the world? Intensely dislike minorities and you will be disposed to ill treat them whatever your political point of view. It is all the more curious that experienced political observers have supposed that being on the ideological left provides some protection against the effects of prejudice, since they are well aware of how limited is the ordinary citizen's understanding of political ideologies.

Figure 3.8 shows the impact of prejudice on the positions that citizens at different points on the ideological spectrum take on an array of questions regarding immigrant minorities. They include making immigration more difficult; taking the position that minorities have more rights than they deserve; and taking the even more extreme position that immigrant minorities are not entitled to equal rights. The impact of prejudice is calculated separately for those on the political left, in the center, and on the political right.[39] Sometimes the power of prejudice is greatest on the right—for example, in promoting opposition to the principle that minorities are entitled to equal rights. Sometimes the impact of prejudice is greatest in the center—for example, in encouraging support for the idea that immigrant minorities now have more rights than they deserve. Sometimes the impact of prejudice is as great on the left as on the right—for example, in promoting opposition to immigration. But at all times the impact of prejudice is

---

[39] The regression coefficients are unstandardized so as not to be biased by different variances within groups, although standardized coefficients, as it happens, give the same finding. All variables are standardized to run from 0 to 1.

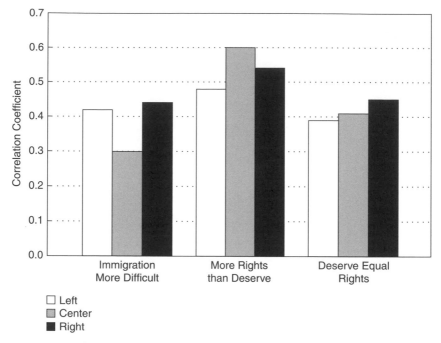

Fig. 3.8. Correlation between prejudice and issue position for the political left, center, and right

powerful on both the left and the right. The view that the threat of prejudice is confined to, or even concentrated on, the right is false. The danger runs right across the political spectrum.

Prejudice is not the only basis of conflict between majority and minority. But all of our findings—on the frequency of negative evaluations of minorities; on their indiscriminateness; on their consistency; and, now, on their impact on citizens across the political spectrum—underline that these other conflicts of identity and values are being played out against a common background of prejudice.

CHAPTER 4

Identity

OBSERVATION OF EVERYDAY LIFE is not a substitute for systematic analysis. But it works the other way around, too: systematic analysis is not a substitute for observation of everyday life. We begin, therefore, with the concerns of actual individuals speaking in their own voice.[1]

THREE VOICES

All the speakers are Dutch, and all live in Rotterdam in neighborhoods where many immigrants live. One woman, giving her sense of what it was like to live there, offered a vignette from her everyday routine: shopping at one of her neighborhood stores. In her words,

> At this shop all people . . . most people who work there are Turkish. And they speak Turkish. It is okay with me if people speak Turkish among themselves, but I hate it that they speak Turkish every time when I am in the shop. Therefore I went to one of these young Turkish speaking guys and I tell him: "Hey listen, I don't want to make a big point of it, but you are in the Netherlands and you work in a Dutch shop, so why shouldn't you speak Dutch?" He answers: "That is none of your business!" So I go to the manager and it appears that they have discussed that many times but without any result and the manager concludes that he can do nothing about it. So I tell him: "Now if

[1] The material is taken from group discussions conducted by Verkuyten.

71

you cannot do anything about it then I will write a complaint to
the owner of the shop because I don't accept it. This is the Netherlands and I am in a Dutch shop, so let them speak Dutch, because it is very unpleasant to walk around there as a Dutch person and you only hear people speaking Turkish.[2]

Language is a sign as well as a medium of identity. The woman does
not complain that the shop workers are inefficient or even that they
speak a different language. On the contrary, she says, "It is okay with
me if people speak Turkish among themselves." It galls her, though,
that they speak Turkish when she is in the shop. This is her country,
not theirs. When she is "in a Dutch shop," they should speak her language, not theirs. She has strong feelings about this: "I hate it that
they speak Turkish every time when I am in the shop." The alienation
is reciprocal, if her report is trustworthy. The response of a Turkish
worker is dismissive, rude: "That is none of your business." And when
she goes to the store manager with her complaint, she experiences a
sense of futility—the manager reports that he is helpless to do anything about it—combined with a sense of shared grievance—many
others have made the same complaint. The complaint is not that she
encounters foreigners in her everyday life; it is that she is made to feel
like a foreigner in her own country.

Here is a second voice, a Dutch man. His complaint is quite different.

These people come here and before they enter the country they
already know where they have to be and when they have arrived
they immediately go to the housing cooperative and they just
announce: "I demand a house!," another discussant adds, "and
otherwise I will stab a knife between your ribs." And the housing cooperative then appears to have a house. But if you come
there as a Dutch person then they say we don't have a house for
you. And then there is social welfare and it is for everybody. But
we don't go there to say that we don't have money enough and
just give me some. But they drive their big Mercedes in front of

---

[2] Verkuyten 1997, 81–82.

the door and just hold their hand out. Everybody knows it, everybody knows it.[3]

The tone is different—angrier (the rhetoric, too), more exaggerated, more stereotypical: "they drive their big Mercedes in front of the door and just hold their hand out." But the deepest difference is in the substance of the complaint. The root problem is not a conflict of cultures; it is a clash of interests.

Immigrant minorities, this man charges, come to the Netherlands for material benefits, such as housing and welfare support. Indeed, they learn how the welfare system works even before they come so that they can exploit it as soon as they arrive. And they are shameless in exploiting its benefits: "[W]hen they have arrived they immediately go the housing cooperative and they just announce: "I demand a house." That is one part of his complaint—and he is genuinely aggrieved. But his deeper grievance is that "they" get these benefits at "our" expense. The housing cooperative says no to the Dutch but yes to the immigrant. It is not only that they are taking what is not theirs. It also is that they are taking it from us: the more they get, the less there is for us to get.

Here is a third speaker, a Dutch mother, with another grievance.

No, you should not say that parents have to teach their children how to deal with immigrant children, no it should be the other way around. Because the Dutch children feel threatened, my daughter feels herself to be threatened in a group of those immigrant children, yes why, because then it is not hands off, my daughter will hit back when it is one other child but not when they are four or five. That is their mentality, they think that that is normal. Just see what happens when you disagree with an immigrant and it gets a little out of hand, then there immediately show up five or ten around you and you will have no chance, no way out and children see that. (Immigrant) children also see that their parents walk around with knives and sticks, or have a big

---

[3] Ibid., 96.

mouth, or what else. If my daughter is not showing respect or swears, now, then she is sent directly up to her room."

She begins by looking through the eyes of her daughter. What she sees is physical aggression. Immigrant children attack her daughter. The grievance here is different from those of the first two speakers. The threat is not to cultural identity or material self-interest; it is to personal safety. Her daughter, she declares, is perfectly capable of taking care of herself in a fair fight: "my daughter will hit back when it is one other child." The problem is that immigrant children gang up. It is not just one child who attacks her daughter; it is four or five. That is why her daughter feels threatened and unable to defend herself. Her mother then strikingly extends this theme of gang attacks. Dutch adults, she maintains, have the same experience as Dutch children: "[W]hen you disagree with an immigrant and it gets a little out of hand, then there immediately show up five or ten around you and you will have no chance, no way out." The concern of the Dutch mother is personal safety in the strongest sense. She refers to immigrants walking around "with knives and sticks." The fear for safety is not her concern alone. Remember the person, listening to the complaint that minorities exploit the welfare system who spontaneously interjected—immigrants say, give me what I want, "otherwise I will stab a knife between your ribs."

These are the concerns we shall explore—that immigrants act as though they still are in "their" country, exploit the welfare system at the expense of the Dutch, and are threats to personal safety. It is necessary now to test their validity systematically.

TWO THEORIES

Social identity theory is currently one of the two most influential theories on group conflict.[4] Individuals, the theory posits, have a need for a positive self-evaluation. To think well of themselves, people need to

---

[4] Tajfel, the creator of social identity theory, was one of the most imaginative as well as influential social psychologists studying group conflict. See, for example, Tajfel 1981.

think well of the groups they belong to. To think well of the groups they belong to, they need to distinguish them from others, putting their group in a light that shines to its advantage and puts other groups in a light that shines to their disadvantage.[5] But if they think less well of other groups in order to think better of their own, they will respond favorably to others they categorize as belonging to the same group as themselves and unfavorably to others they categorize as belonging to a different group than themselves.

The "minimal group" experiments dramatically illustrate the importance of group categorization.[6] Here is an example of a minimal group. Some people are told, on a purely random basis of course, that they have counted more dots than there are in a picture; others are told that they have counted fewer dots. Everyone then is asked to allocate rewards to others. All they know of the others is that they are either an "over-" or an "under-" counter of dots. They then favor those who made the same mistake as they, at the expense of those who made the opposite mistake—*even though this means minimizing the total award to their own group.*

"Over-counters" and "under-counters" are the most minimal groups conceivable.[7] Their members are unknown to each other; they have no common history; they will share no common future; they are organized only on the basis of a single characteristic that is of no importance. Yet, categorizing others as the same as or different from oneself in a completely unimportant respect is sufficient to induce a bias in favor of one's own group at the expense of the other.

There is an insight of originality and power in social identity theory.[8] But it has had an odd fate. There now are two versions of it, and

[5] Robinson 1996, 16.

[6] The research literature on minimal groups is enormous. For the classic presentation, see Tajfel 1981.

[7] One index of the strain on social identity theory is that this interpretation is now being turned upside down: rather than minimal groups, as they have been characterized for a generation, they now are characterized as "maximal-group experiments." See Reicher 2004, 929–30.

[8] A fascinating part of social identity theory, which we regrettably cannot draw on because of the restriction of our principal sample to members of the majority group, is its exploration of an array of strategic responses of minorities. See Tajfel 1978.

though both are asserted to be consistent with the theory, each is inconsistent with the other. The first version asserts that the mere act of categorization generates bias in favor of the in-group.[9] And if totally fictitious groups can command the loyalty of their members, one can only imagine the power of groups that draw on the force of tradition, shared experience, socialization, common institutions, and the full apparatus of symbolic loyalties and socialized identities. The second version asserts that what is crucial is not categorization but the context in which people are categorized.[10] In the jargon, positive evaluative contexts lead to positive bonds between groups; negative evaluative contexts, to negative ones. By itself, the second argument runs, categorization is as likely "to produce friendship and spontaneous respect as rejection and discrimination" as in-group favoritism and out-group bias.[11]

The first version offers a warning against policies that highlight differences in group identity, multiculturalism being a paradigmatic example. The second version turns the cautionary lesson of the first on its head. Multiculturalism as public policy entails public categorization of groups. But what counts in the second version is not categorization per se but the evaluative context in which categorization occurs. And the aim of multiculturalism is precisely to promote positive evaluative contexts.

Happily, it is not necessary for us to decide between the two versions; both yield the same prediction for the particular problem we are grappling with. Our concern is with what happens when issues of identity are brought to the fore, not in a context that psychological experimenters can ensure is positive, but in a context that characteristically is negative—the battles of real politics—precisely because no one has the degree of power to ensure that it is positive, and the prospect of important losses favors the chances that it is negative.

The second of the two major theories, realistic conflict theory, focuses on self-interest. Its premise is that economic resources are scarce,

[9] Note Turner's (1996) uncontentious presentation of the claim.
[10] Oakes and Haslam 2001, 183; see also Reicher 2004.
[11] All, and many others, cited in Oakes and Haslam 2001.

as are the means of obtaining them. Competition is unavoidable and, what is more, is rational.

This idea that if "they" have more "we" have less was at the heart of the second speaker's grievance about immigrants exploiting the Dutch welfare system, leaving less for the Dutch.[12] It also is at the core of the third speaker's concern about immigrants ganging up to attack Dutch, for nothing is more in the self-interest of an individual than his own safety. Realistic conflict theory comes in different flavors, depending on precisely what assumptions are made.[13] Some put the fundamental emphasis on tangible, economic self-interest; others have a more expansive conception of self-interest covering social status, even including privileges in "areas of intimacy and privacy."[14] Our tests cover both. Some flavors of realistic conflict theory have strict rationality requirements; others are slacker. Our tests are midway between the poles, requiring not that individuals make optimal choices given their objective circumstances, but that they make choices consistent with their perception of their circumstances. Finally, some versions of realistic conflict theory posit that the fundamental level of competition is between individuals; others, that it is between groups. For our purposes, what is important is that individuals can see their self-interest at risk at either an individual or group level, or both. Our Dutch mother made the point. She was worried about the personal safety of her daughter, but she also was concerned that Dutch in general face a similar danger. So, too, with economic self-interest. A person can be concerned that he will be economically worse off, that the society as a whole will be worse off, or both.

---

[12] It is curious, and worth remarking, that under the theory of realistic conflict actors do not calculate that everyone can be better-off, for example, through an expanding economy.

[13] The paradigmatic examples of these polar contracts are, on the one side, Hardin 1995, who develops the theoretically most strict and therefore most powerful version of rational choice theory, and Blumer's classic (1958) analysis. See Bobo and Hutchings 1996; Bobo and Garcia 1992; Bobo 1999; and Bobo 1983, who develop a more sociological version of realistic conflict theory. For example, Blumer includes resources, statuses, and privileges for the in-group understood in the broadest terms, for example, including "areas of intimacy and privacy" (Blumer 1958, 4). For a contrasting objective conception of group interests, see Quillian 1995, 1996.

[14] Blumer 1958, 4.

The versions of realistic conflict theory now on the table have, we believe, at least one perverse feature and possibly two. The first perverse feature is this: The strength of the approach is its sensitivity to differences of interests. It is all the more puzzling, then, that applications of the theory to prejudice and politics pass over conflicts of interests *within* the majority. And there manifestly are conflicts of interests within the majority on immigration. Some fear that they will be worse off because of immigrant minorities. But others in the majority—including many of the most influential in the majority—believe that they and the society at large will be better-off. Leaders of opinion in politics and business argue—often sincerely—that cultural diversity is a benefit. More fundamentally, they see the economic benefits of immigration as undeniable. The native population is aging; its birthrate is declining; yet the levels of the society's social benefits are staying the same. There now are, or soon will be, too few in the labor force to sustain a welfare state on the European model. It is in the economic interest of the majority—indeed, may be an economic necessity—to import more labor from other countries.[15] And under all scenarios, importing low-skill labor threatens some in the majority more than others; indeed, under most scenarios, many in the majority not only will not suffer from it but will prosper by it.

The second perverse feature of realistic conflict theories, applied to analyses of the politics of immigrant minorities, is that they ignore minorities.[16] Immigrant minorities sometimes are characterized as pliant; rarely as aggressive; nearly always as passive bystanders—in any case, marginal to an understanding of the strains between majority

[15] Perhaps it is worth noting as an aside that there are political as well as economic gains to be had. Political gains and losses also are part of the competing interests *within* the majority. It already is in the electoral interest of some major political parties to align themselves with the cause of minorities, in the interest of others to challenge it, and is likely to be still more so in the future.

[16] A notable exception is the work of Bobo et al. 2000. In general, though, attention to the role of minorities is one of the major points of difference between social identity and realistic conflict theories. Paradoxically, the strategic reactions of minorities have been a major concern for the former, not the latter—an intriguing anomaly of a psychological approach taking rational choice more seriously than an ostensibly realistic conflict approach.

and minority. The majority determines whether there will be conflict, what degree of conflict there will be, and what terms the conflict will be fought out on. Of course, there is an obvious rationale for focusing on the majority. An established majority, because it is both established and a majority, has more power than a minority. But because it is sensible to acknowledge that a minority has less power than a majority, it does not make it less odd to proceed as though minorities play no role in determining whether there will be a conflict and, odder still, to tacitly assume that they do not have the means to influence the terms of a conflict. Muslims in the Netherlands have clearly demonstrated that they do.

BRINGING THE TWO THEORIES TOGETHER

Motives are explanations twice over—the reason, from the perspective of an actor, for his choice of a course of action; the meaning, from the perspective of an observer, of the course of action an actor has chosen. The two are deeply connected. Our understanding of why some in the majority want to exclude immigrant minorities depends on their reasons for wanting to do so. If it is because they are concerned about being economically worse off, we shall have one understanding of what the conflict is about—and, possibly, what may be done to relieve strains between majority and minority. On the other hand, if they are reacting negatively to immigrant minorities because they are concerned that their own cultural identity is threatened, we have a quite different understanding of what the conflict is about—and what, if anything, may be done to overcome it. Of course, it is not a matter of either economic self-interest or concerns about cultural identity. Both realistic conflict and social identity theories throw light on why people are reacting as they are. The question is, does one throw a good deal more light than the other?

Native Dutch workers who are employed in low-skill jobs are more threatened by immigrant job seekers than those employed in high-skill occupations. Of course, to put conflicts of interest in these terms presumes that what matters are people's objective circumstances. But there is no one-to-one correspondence between people's objective circumstances and their perceptions of their circumstances. Some perceive the competitive threat; others similarly situated do not. It follows that it is not the reality of competition that counts; it is "[a] *perception* that the out-group wishes to increase its share of valued resources and statuses at the expense of the in-group."[17] Hence the need to focus on *perceived*, as against actual, competitive threats.[18]

It is the distinctive contribution of Bobo and Hutchings to have developed a technique to measure perceived threat. Subsequent research has followed their measurement template.[19] In evaluating their technique we accordingly are assessing the whole stream of research on perceived threat. The following is a list of the components of their measure.[20]

- *Job competition:* More good jobs for (Asians/blacks/Hispanics) means fewer good jobs for members of other groups.
- *Political competition:* The more influence (Asians/blacks/Hispanics) have in local politics the less influence members of other groups will have in local politics.
- *Housing competition:* As more good housing and neighborhoods go to (Asians/blacks/Hispanics), the fewer good housing and neighborhoods there will be for members of other groups.
- *Economic competition:* Many (Asians/blacks/Hispanics) have been trying to get ahead economically at the expense of other groups.

Each refers to an object of value—good jobs, good housing and neighborhoods, political influence, economic advancement—then each asks whether more for one group means less for others.

Here is a thought experiment. You join two neighbors in the middle of a conversation. One confides in you. Taking in immigrant minori-

---

[17] Bobo and Hutchings 1996; emphasis added.

[18] Blalock 1967.

[19] We follow here Scheepers, Gijsbers, and Coenders 2002 because of the clarity of their presentation. The lines of argument, though, are standard.

[20] Bobo and Hutchings 1996, 958.

noise, who is hammering, and I look outside, and there sits this monkey, this little Moroccan, sits there with a bike lock that is rusted and puts de-rusting oil on it, and is hammering on it." When we try to hear him speak these words, not just read them on the printed page, we hear first the hate—"there sits this monkey, this little Moroccan." The concern about crime is expressed strikingly—"they steal bikes like a magpie." But the hate is primary, the threat of crime secondary—a consequence of the hate; certainly not the cause of it. If we asked Rob the standard question of whether he perceived minorities to pose a threat to crime, his answer would be yes—but not because his sense of security has been shaken but because he cannot abide Moroccans. The problem is clear. To the degree that measures of threat perception simultaneously measure feelings of hostility toward a group, they are measuring the very thing they are intended to explain. Perceptions of a threat from minorities will then be observed to go hand in hand with hostility to minorities. But that is because what is supposed to be doing the explaining—hostility to minorities—is the same thing as what is being explained—hostility to minorities. This is not a discovery. It is a tautology.

A PROPOSED SOLUTION

This is a tangle. We would like to take a step back from the practical problem of measurement to consider why the concept of threat is potentially a useful explanatory construct.

The analytical role of perceived threat is to specify the drivers of group conflict. Is it a function of perceived threats to an individual's economic well-being? To their status? Or perhaps to something else altogether? The heart of a realistic conflict explanation is to pick out who is threatened by what. It is therefore all the harder to follow why those who emphasize the role of threat perceptions as a source of hostility between groups have followed the practice they have. They first measure different threats that a majority may perceive a minority poses. But then, rather than distinguishing between the threats, to see

ties has provided a pool of cheap labor; already it has cost some of her friends their jobs; now she fears it threatens hers. The second neighbor joins in, agreeing that immigrants threaten a lot of people's jobs and, what is more, immigrants suck up government assistance, costing Dutch society more and more each year, and—what is more again—have driven up the crime rate.

You have known both neighbors for a long time. Previously the first did not complain about immigrants—indeed, this neighbor had expressed some sympathy toward them and their problems. The second has complained about immigrant minorities for as long as you have known him. Asked if immigrants threaten jobs for the Dutch, both your neighbors would agree. But although they are saying the same thing, they don't mean the same thing. The first neighbor has come to feel that her job is at risk and therefore feels herself to be threatened. The second has always disliked almost everything about minorities—their talking a foreign language in public, their offensive behavior, the odd clothes they wear, and so on and so forth. Both neighbors are critical of immigrant minorities. But they differ in a key respect. One perceives that immigrants pose an economic threat; the other dislikes them pure and simple. The question is, using the standard approach, could you tell them apart?

The standard approach has an obvious problem. Each question may measure *both* whether you think something you value is at risk and how you feel about a particular group. But that opens up two quite different reasons for agreeing that there is a threat. You may agree because you see that particular group as a threat and therefore dislike it. Alternatively, you may perceive that group poses a threat because you dislike it. In the first alternative, perception of a threat is the cause and hostility to the group the effect. In the second alternative, it is just the other way around: hostility to the group is the cause and perception of a threat the effect.[21]

Which is cause and which is effect? Recall Rob: "That Moroccan family next door was back home again, they steal bikes like a magpie, they bring their friends in for it and last week or so I think, what is that

[21] Bobo and Hutchings 1996.

which matters more, which less, they do just the opposite. They add up, for each individual, the number of ways that he or she feels threatened. *The more ways that people perceive themselves to be threatened, the more threatened they perceive themselves to be.*

It is hard to follow their reasoning. Researchers who focus on threats mean real threats. The aim is to account for hostility between groups on the basis of real competition between them to be better-off or have a higher standing. But what is the competition about? Is it about being better-off economically? Having a higher standing in society? Safety? A group's way of life? Depending on which is the dominant factor in any particular case, we can have a quite different understanding of what the conflict between groups is actually about. But rather than picking out the specific factor that is driving a particular conflict, the standard procedure accomplishes just the opposite. It adds up the number of threats a person perceives, whatever he perceives is threatened, thereby building a measure of the degree to which people have a *generalized susceptibility* to feel threatened. Thus Bobo and Hutchings meant to measure perception of specific threats; they instead measured a diffuse feeling of being threatened—not the same thing at all and not at all what they set out to do. They meant to reject a psychological approach and put forward a sociological one. They have more nearly done the reverse.

Differentiation is the key. The problem with speaking of conflicts of "interests" and "identity" is less that they are abstract but more that they are vague. Two ways of interpreting the notion of "interests" stand out—the first being economic interests, and the second the most fundamental interest of all, safety. As for identity, since it is the reaction of the majority group to minorities that we are investigating, it is (perceived) threats to its cultural identity that we should focus on.

Our focus is thus on three types of threat. But two of the three can present themselves at two different levels. People may be concerned about their personal economic well-being without being worried about the economic well-being of the society as a whole. Alternatively, they may be concerned about the economic well-being of the society as a whole, without feeling that they themselves are at risk. Or, of course, they may perceive a threat at both levels. The same is true of the most fundamental of "interests"—safety. A person may be worried about violence and vandalism in his or her own neighborhood without seeing them as a threat to the society as a whole. Alternatively, people may be worried about the level of violence and vandalism in the society as a whole without being concerned that they themselves are in danger. Or, again, they can perceive a threat at both levels. By contrast, a threat to cultural identity can be perceived only at the collective level. Economic well-being, safety, collective identity—three types of threats, two of which may come at two levels, individual and collective: five in all.

THE DECOUPLING EXPERIMENT

Previous research on threat perception has used one question to measure two different things: perceiving that an object of value is at risk and disliking the group that allegedly is putting it at risk. The solution is to decouple the two.

In one condition of the "decoupling" experiment, threat is measured as it is standardly done: the object at risk and the group posing the risk are coupled together. For example, a randomly selected half of the sample is asked whether they agree or disagree with the following statement: "I am afraid of increasing violence and vandalism in my neighborhood by ethnic minorities."[22] By contrast, in the test condition the other half of the sample is asked whether they agree with exactly the same statement—whether they are afraid of increasing violence and vandalism in their neighborhood—but the reference to ethnic minorities is omitted.

The top panel of this list sets out the five threat questions in the "coupled" condition; the bottom panel wording is in the "decoupled" condition.

---

[22] The response format is modified Likert. Four response options are offered: strongly agree; somewhat agree; somewhat disagree; strongly disagree.

Threat Items: "Coupled" Condition

Individual Safety Threat
  "I am afraid of increasing violence and vandalism in my neighbor-
  hood by ethnic minorities."
Individual Economic Threat
  "I am afraid that my economic prospects will get worse because of
  ethnic minorities."
Collective Safety Threat
  "I am afraid of increasing violence and vandalism in Dutch society
  by ethnic minorities."
Collective Economic Threat
  "I am afraid that the economic prospects of Dutch society will get
  worse because of minorities."
Collective Cultural Threat
  "These days, I am afraid that the Dutch culture is threatened by
  ethnic minorities."

Threat Items: "Decoupled" Condition

Individual Safety Threat
  "I am afraid of increasing violence and vandalism in my neighbor-
  hood."
Individual Economic Threat
  "I am afraid that my economic prospects will get worse."
Collective Safety Threat
  "I am afraid of increasing violence and vandalism in Dutch society."
Collective Economic Threat
  "I am afraid that the economic prospects of Dutch society will get
  worse."
Collective Cultural Threat
  "These days, I am afraid that the Dutch culture is threatened."

What should we observe if standard threat perception measures
confound what is to be explained with what is supposed to be pro-
viding the explanation? One implication is this: When a threat and a

minority group posing the threat are coupled, then the more that people dislike minorities, the more likely they should be to agree that they pose a threat *whatever is purportedly threatened*. And so far as this is so, then in the "coupled" condition answers to each threat question should be highly correlated with answers to every other threat. In contrast, when the threat and the group purportedly posing the threat are decoupled, the pattern of correlations should be differentiated. For example, people who are afraid of increasing violence and vandalism in their neighborhood should also be more likely to be concerned about increasing violence and vandalism in Dutch society; those who are concerned about the economic prospects of Dutch society should also be more likely to be concerned about their own economic prospects.

Table 4.1 presents the intercorrelations of threat perception indicators in the coupled condition above the diagonal; in the decoupled condition, below the diagonal. As inspection of table 4.1 shows, threat judgments are markedly more correlated with one another—whatever is threatened—above the diagonal than below. The median correlation between threats in the coupled condition is .49; in the decoupled condition, .24. Mentioning minorities has the effect of maximizing the similarity of the threats; not mentioning them has the effect of maximizing the distinctiveness of threats.

These results suggest that questions in the standard format that appear to be asking different questions—one about safety, another about economic well-being, and so on—to a substantial degree are versions of the same questions. What is threatened is different, but every threat has a reference to minorities. The problem is obvious. The results in table 4.1 suggest that the standard threat measures are not only measuring whether people dislike minorities because they perceive them to pose a threat to something they value. The "threat" measures also are picking up whether people dislike minorities. But this is the same as saying that they are explaining whether people dislike minorities by measuring in another way whether they dislike minorities. There is no explanation, only tautology.

How serious is the risk of tautology with standard threat perception measures? If they are measures of whether people dislike minorities, whatever else they also measure, then each threat measure

TABLE 4.1
Correlations of Threat Measures Coupled above the Diagonal, Decoupled below the Diagonal

	Individual safety threat	Individual economic threat	Collective safety threat	Collective economic threat	Collective cultural threat
Individual safety threat		.41 (1007)	.48 (1011)	.38 (1004)	.39 (999)
Individual economic threat	.19 (972)		.43 (1008)	.59 (1002)	.52 (996)
Collective safety threat	.38 (983)	.11 (972)		.56 (1005)	.57 (1000)
Collective economic threat	.20 (971)	.41 (963)	.20 (971)		.64 (995)
Collective cultural threat	.28 (961)	.19 (950)	.29 (961)	.40 (950)	

Number of observations in parentheses. Coupled median = .49
Decoupled median = .24

should be as good a predictor of hostility toward minorities as every other. And so far as this is so, then the standard threat measures generate tautologies, not explanations.

Table 4.2 shows how well each of the five threat measures predicts hostility toward minorities, first when minorities are mentioned in the threat question, then when they are not.[23] Look first at the results when minorities are mentioned (column 1). Perceiving a threat to personal safety contributes significantly to hostility. The same holds true for a threat to personal economic well-being and for every other kind of threat—violence and vandalism in the society as a whole; the economic well-being of the society as a whole; and the national culture. What's more, with the exception of a threat to personal safety, the impact of

---

[23] See Sniderman, Hagendoorn, and Prior 2004 for more detailed analysis.

Table 4.2

Regression of Stereotype Hostility to Minorities on Threats

	Total Prejudice	
	Coupled	*Decoupled*
Constant	.12***	.11***
	(.01)	(.03)
Individual safety	.06***	.04
	1.47	*1.26*
	(.02)	(.02)
Individual economic threat	.14***	.09***
	1.76	*1.24*
	(.03)	(.02)
Collective safety threat	.14***	.07*
	1.89	*1.29*
	(.02)	(.03)
Collective economic threat	.14***	.08**
	2.20	*1.42*
	(.03)	(.02)
Collective cultural threat	.13***	.23***
	2.08	*1.31*
	(.02)	(.02)
Adj. R²	.49	.24
N	855	810

***$p < .001$ **$p < .01$, *$p < .05$. Estimated using OLS. Standard errors in parentheses. Variance inflation factors in italics.

every threat is as large as that of every other. Everything matters as much as everything else; which is to say nothing matters in particular.

Remove the overlay of feelings toward minorities, however, and the picture comes into focus (column 2). Some threats count for a lot; others for scarcely anything; and the pattern altogether both surprises and informs. Consider the most elemental threat—to safety. Media reports of rising crime have become common, as well as reports linking the rise in crime to minorities. Judging by media coverage and, for that matter, social conversation, one should expect that concern over crime and vandalism is a major spur to hostility to minorities. Common sense suggests that a concern about a loss of safety—one's own or in the society as a whole—adds a layer of hostility toward minorities on top of the hostility that would be there in any case. Common sense, however, is only half right. A fear of increasing violence and vandalism in one's own neighborhood is not a significant predictor of systematic intolerance of minorities. A fear of increasing violence and vandalism in Dutch society as a whole is.

Although we were interested in the impact of concerns about safety, from the beginning we thought the heart of the matter was conflicts of identity and interests. Which is the primary driver of hostility to minorities? Is it a conflict of interests? Or a conflict of identities? The beginnings of an answer are in table 4.2. Threats to individual economic well-being matter, as do threats to the economic well-being of the society as a whole. But threats to cultural identity matter markedly more. The impact of a threat to cultural identity is roughly two times as big as the impact of any other threat.[24]

One set of results for a measure of prejudice is one thing. Table 4.3 replicates the analysis substituting the social distance measure of prejudice for the stereotype measure. Since threat perceptions are confounded with prejudice when the threat is coupled with a reference to minorities, here and throughout we now analyze those who were in the decoupled condition.

The overall pattern is one of similarity. The threat of violence and vandalism whether to the individual herself or in the society as a whole has no significant connection to intolerance of minorities measured in terms of social distance. But again a threat to an individual's economic well-being increases systematic hostility to minorities as

---

[24] We appreciate that one might reasonably argue that the two measures of economic threat should be combined to capture the total effect of economic self-interest. That might be a compelling argument if they had the same predictors, but they do not. See table 4.4.

TABLE 4.3
Regression of Social Distance Measure of
Prejudice toward Minorities on Threats

Constant	.11***
	(.02)
Individual safety	−.04
	(.02)
Individual economic threat	.09***
	(.02)
Collective safety threat	.07
	(.03)
Collective economic threat	.08**
	(.02)
Collective cultural threat	.23***
	(.02)
Adj. R²	.24
N	810

***$p < .001$ **$p < .01$ *$p < .05$.
Estimated using OLS. Standard errors in
parentheses.

does a threat to the economic well-being of the society as a whole.
And again a threat to the national culture has a markedly greater impact than that of any other threat.

DIGGING BELOW THE SURFACE

Social science is like poker in one respect: a reluctance to quit when
one is ahead can be costly. It is unlike poker in another: face up, the
value of a poker card—its suit and value—is beyond doubt. By con-

trast, the meaning of an answer to a question in an interview—what it actually measures—often is not obvious on its face.

Threats to cultural identity, our analyses show, have a far larger impact on hostility to minorities than any other kind of threat. But what does it actually mean when someone says that he is concerned that the national culture is threatened? It is likely that it means, in part, what it means on its face. But it is unlikely that it *only* means what it means on its face. Here is an obvious hypothesis. Some people lack confidence in their capacity to cope with everyday problems; to hold their own against those around them; or to be the person they wish to be. To the degree that they lack self-esteem, they should be more likely to perceive themselves to be threatened, as it were, on all fronts.[25] So far as this is right, their responses to the measures of perceived threat reveal not whether something in their environment is threatening but their susceptibility to perceiving that something in their environment threatens them—whether it does or not.

Here is a less obvious hypothesis. Suppose a person perceives a threat to the economic prospects of the society. Possibly, his concern follows from tracking the overall performance of the economy. But his concern may track his personal experience, either of doing less well than he used to or fearing that he will not do as well as he has become used to. On this reasoning, when asked a question about the society's economic prospects, he expresses concern to add weight to the concerns he has about his own situation—others are in the same boat, as it were. But in either case, though he *says* he is concerned about the society as a whole, his concern is about himself.

Here is a still less obvious hypothesis. Our initial findings indicate that both threats to cultural identity and economic interests matter, though the former appears to matter markedly more than the latter. But surely it is possible that people are representing their concerns in a way that puts them in the best possible light—as citizens who care about the values and institutions of their society, not just the amount of money they put into their own pockets. Expressing concern about the society's way of life has a high-minded sound to it; doing the same

---

[25] See, in particular, the pioneering study of Marcus et al. 1995.

about your own pocketbook a crass one. But to the extent that they are, as it were, dressing up their answers, our findings are systematically misleading. A concern about cultural identity is being credited with some of the explanatory force that more properly belongs to a concern about economic interests.

We need some way to catch sight of what lies behind the threats that our respondents say that they are concerned about. The approach we shall take is this: If they say that they are concerned about a threat to economic interests, and they mean what they say, then a strong vein of concern about economic matters should be evident in other responses they gave. Alternatively, if they say they are concerned about a threat to the national culture, and they mean what they say, then we should find that a vein of concern about national identity stands out.

Table 4.4 shows how successfully we can predict concern about a particular threat by taking account of three sets of factors—pessimism about economic prospects;[26] the importance of national identity;[27] and their level of self-esteem.[28] We concentrate on the three types of threats that contribute to hostility to minorities—threats to an individual's economic well-being, to the economic well-being of the society as whole, and to the national culture.

There are times when the most important discovery that can be made is the most obvious one that can be made; this is one of those

---

[26] There are two measures. One reflects people's judgments regarding whether their economic situation has gotten worse over the last two years, is likely to do so over the next two, or both. The other reflects their judgments regarding whether the economic situation of the country has gotten worse over the last two years, is likely to do so over the next two, or both.

[27] To assess the importance of national identity to individuals' personal identity, we adapt an index developed by Luhtanen and Crocker 1992. Our measure of national identity combines responses to three statements: "I am often aware that I am Dutch"; "I see myself as a typical Dutch person"; and "I am proud to be Dutch." Alpha = .62.

[28] This is a five-item measure, based on the California Psychological Inventory (CPI), developed for our studies in Western Europe. It consists of responses to the following statements: "When in a group of people, I usually do what others want rather than make suggestions"; "I would have been more successful if people had given me a fair chance"; "I certainly feel useless at times"; "Teachers often expect too much from their students"; and "I frequently wonder what hidden reason another person may have for doing something nice for me." CPI items are designed to be minimally intercorrelated.

TABLE 4.4
Predicting Different Threats

	Collective cultural threat	Individual economic threat	Collective economic threat	Individual safety threat	Collective safety threat
Personal finances two years ago	.12 (.12)	.53*** (.13)	.08 (.12)	−.20 (.12)	−.27 (.14)
Personal finances in two years	.24* (.12)	1.39*** (.13)	.43*** (.12)	.23 (.12)	.20 (.14)
National finances two years ago	.51*** (.10)	.20 (.11)	.82*** (.10)	.09 (.10)	.28* (.12)
National finances in two years	.23* (.12)	.54*** (.12)	1.05*** (.12)	.07 (.12)	.20 (.13)
Dutch identity	1.25*** (.14)	.46** (.15)	.64*** (.14)	.60*** (.14)	.59*** (.15)
Self-esteem	−.78*** (.21)	−1.05*** (.21)	−.81*** (.20)	−.58** (.20)	−.48* (.24)
1st cut point	−.29	.50	.18	−.63	−1.52
2nd cut point	.28	1.23	1.03	−.24	−1.20
3rd cut point	1.04	1.99	1.86	.36	−.33
L-likelihood	−1122.70	−930.57	−1075.45	−1193.69	−805.56
N	885	900	898	905	906

***$p < .001$ **$p < .01$ *$p < .05$.
Estimated using ordered probit. Standard errors in parentheses. Sample is unweighted.

times. The question is: When people report that they believe there is a threat to the national culture, is that really what they are concerned about? Or does some other concern lie behind their words? To have confidence that when people say they are concerned about threats to cultural identity they mean what they say, we need the most direct evidence possible, which is just what table 4.4 provides. Far and away the strongest predictor of perceived threat to the Dutch culture is the importance of being Dutch to a person's sense of personal identity.

The other lesson in table 4.4 goes deeper. From one angle, posing questions in terms of antitheses—is it economic interests or is it cultural identity?—clarifies the explanatory alternatives. From another, it has just the opposite effect of obscuring the explanatory alternatives. Asking which of the two—self-interest or identity—is the more important assumes that they are unrelated: that one cannot be concerned about the economic well-being of the country because one is concerned about the national culture, and the other way around. But as table 4.4 shows, the two are entangled. One root of a concern that the Dutch culture is threatened is a concern that the economic prospects of Dutch society and—to a lesser extent—those of the individual herself will deteriorate. It may, on first hearing, sound surprising that pessimism about the national economy is a reason why people perceive that the national culture is threatened. It did not catch us by surprise—but only because we did not have the wit to think of the possibility in advance. After the fact, it seems reasonable that those who think their country is badly off in one way are more likely to think it is badly off in another.

This result may suggest that concerns about culture are epiphenomenal and that concerns about self-interest are the real driving force. So many favor this line of reasoning because it sounds so plausible. On their face, economic interests are the most hardboiled component of a causal explanation; and perceived economic threats have roots in people's economic circumstances—or, more precisely, their judgment of their economic prospects and those of the society as a whole. But they are also deeply rooted in noneconomic considerations.

Two consistent patterns stand out in table 4.4. The first is that people who lack self-confidence are more likely to perceive threats on all fronts—to the national culture, to their economic prospects, to those of the society as a whole, to their individual safety, and to that of the society as a whole. This is a result with a sting for those who believe that economic self-interest is the fundamental driving force of human choice. Economic reality can underlie psychological perceptions. But, equally, ostensibly economic judgments are sometimes actually psychological ones.

The second consistent pattern is the role of national identity. The more important being Dutch is to a person, the more likely he or she is to perceive threats on all fronts and, as we have seen, to be more intolerant of immigrant minorities. Concerns about identity are the consistent thread that runs through our findings. We have seen they matter for people who are concerned about a threat to their cultural identity. We shall see now that issues of identity also matter for those who are not concerned about them.

Many people are concerned that the Dutch culture is at risk. But a large number are not. They disagree that their cultural identity is threatened. The question we want to ask is: How will they react when for whatever reason the issue of cultural identity becomes salient?

From a political point of view, two alternatives stand out. Bringing issues of identity to the fore may *galvanize* those already concerned about them. It may also *mobilize* citizens who ordinarily are not concerned about them. The politics of the two alternatives differ profoundly. Galvanizing a core constituency increases the intensity of concern in a segment of the electorate, but it provides incentives to respond only for politicians who depend on that constituency. Mobilization reaches beyond the core constituency; hence it provides incentives for a larger set of politicians to respond.

PROBLEMS OF CULTURAL AND ECONOMIC INTEGRATION

Those who are concerned about their economic well-being, as we have seen, tend to be more hostile to immigrants and opposed to immigration; those who are concerned about threats to their cultural identity are still more so. We now want to explore a different question:

To what extent can people be induced to take exclusionary positions by making issues of economic well-being or cultural identity salient?

To get leverage on this question, we carried out the "fitting in" experiment.[29] In this exercise, potential immigrants are sometimes described in favorable terms, sometimes in unfavorable ones. Respondents are randomly assigned to one of four conditions. In the first and second, "a group of new immigrants that may come here" is characterized either as "highly educated and well suited for well-paying jobs" or as "not highly educated or well trained and only suited for unskilled jobs." In the third and fourth conditions, immigrants are characterized either as people who "speak Dutch fluently and have a very good chance to fit in smoothly with the Dutch culture" or as people who "don't speak Dutch fluently and don't have a good chance to fit in smoothly with the Dutch culture." All are asked the same test item: "Do you think it is a good idea or bad idea for these immigrants to be allowed to come here?"

Which evokes the stronger reaction—the problem of cultural integration or that of economic integration? Figure 4.1 reports the distribution of responses (from immigration being an extremely bad idea through it being an extremely good idea). The top part of the figure shows differences in reaction between immigrants that are likely to fit in well culturally and those who will not; the other part shows differences in reaction between immigrants that are likely to fit in well economically and those who are not.

Plainly, people balk when problems of either cultural or economic integration are brought into the foreground: it would be surprising if they are as likely to welcome immigrants who were going to pose a problem as those who would readily fit in. The relevant finding is that problems of cultural integration dominate those of economic integration. Expressed in terms of a summary correlation, the association between a problem of cultural integration and opposition is .39; the association between a problem of economic integration and opposition is .17. The results for situational triggers thus parallel those for dispositional concerns. Issues of identity are the button to push if politicians want to press for an advantage on issues of minorities.

[29] See also Hagendoorn and Sniderman 2001.

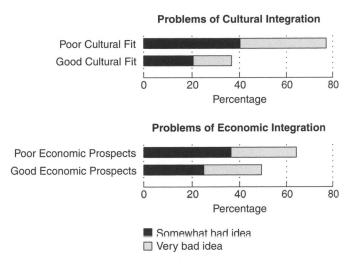

Fig. 4.1. "New immigrants a bad idea?"

Still, there is a political calculus to be worked out. If politicians bring to the fore problems of minorities integrating culturally (or economically, for that matter), who will respond? Those who are already concerned about the cultural identity of the country? Or a wider circle, including those who ordinarily do not think there is any reason to be concerned about the national identity?

A person's national identity goes deep. Our intuition is this: Many people are not concerned about a threat to their cultural identity. But they will react if their attention is directed to it. They will not wind up as strongly in favor of an exclusionary response as a person who already is concerned about these issues, since they start off much less likely to favor one. But they will react as strongly.

The first column of Table 4.5 presents the results of taking into account three factors: (1) a preexisting concern about cultural identity; (2) making the problem of cultural integration salient; (3) the interaction, if any, between the two. The impact of both predisposition and situational trigger is significant, which is not surprising. The key question is whether the two interact. If increasing the salience of the issue of cultural integration has a galvanizing effect, then respondents more concerned about a threat to the national culture should be

TABLE 4.5

"Immigration a Bad Idea" Regressed on Predispositions and Triggers

	Cultural trigger	Economic trigger (collective)	Economic trigger (individual)
Constant	.30***	.40***	.46***
	(.03)	(.03)	(.03)
Predisposition	.26***	.29***	.16***
	(.05)	(.05)	(.05)
Trigger	.19***	.19***	.11***
	(.05)	(.04)	(.04)
Trigger * Predisposition	.03	-.10	.07
	(.07)	(.07)	(.07)
Adj. R²	.21	.13	.09
N	444	492	496

***$p < .001$ **$p < .01$ *$p < .05$.

Estimated using OLS. Standard errors in parentheses.

disproportionately more likely to oppose immigration—that is, there will be a significant interaction. By contrast, if triggering a concern about cultural integration has a mobilizing effect, it should evoke proportionately as strong a reaction across the board—that is, there should be no interaction between perception of cultural threat and the experimental treatment. And there is not. Here is where a negative finding is more revealing than a positive one. The absence of an interaction means that those who do not agree at all that Dutch culture is threatened react as strongly to problems of cultural integration as those who are most concerned that it is threatened.

We test the robustness of this result by parallel analysis of economic integration: the second column analyzes the possible interplay of concern about a threat to the economy as a whole and a problem of economic integration becoming salient; the third, the possible interplay of a concern about a threat to an individual's own economic prospects and a problem of economic integration. For both, a preexisting concern increases the likelihood of an exclusionary reaction, as before. Also for both, a problem of economic integration becoming salient also does so, as before. But again, the key question is how those who were not concerned at all about an economic threat react. Do they give less weight to issues of economic integration when they become salient than do those who are very concerned about them? And again, the answer is the same whether the concern is about the economy as a whole or the individual's own economic prospects.

Threats to cultural identity, all of our findings indicate, are more likely to evoke exclusionary reactions than threats to economic self-interest. But threats to either, our findings also make plain, evoke exclusionary reactions. Concerns about cultural and economic integration of course are not mutually exclusive. Circumstances, and politics, can make either or both salient. And the effect of making either salient is to mobilize opposition to immigrants and immigration throughout the society, not merely to galvanize it in segments already concerned about threats to economic well-being and, still more so, to cultural identity. Here, we believe, is a key to the "flash" potential of the politics of both identity and self-interest.

CHAPTER 5

Top-Down Politics

EVERYTHING IS WHAT IT IS and not something else—a truism in logic but (often) an illusion in politics. *Inspraak* is the Dutch word for the practice of consultation. Nominally, inspraak is a way to involve citizens in the formulation of public policies. Ministers and their civil servants consult with citizens, neighborhood organizations, and citizen groups potentially affected by a proposed policy; then, with the views of the public in hand, they reevaluate and, where necessary, amend the proposed policy. This consultation carousel has two aims— publicly (and secondarily) to facilitate representation of citizens' views; privately (and primarily) to legitimate policy decisions of governmental elites.[1]

TWO MODELS OF POLITICS

Analyses of public opinion and politics broadly follow a common line. Political cleavages in the electorate, the story runs, are rooted in deeper cleavages within the larger society—between economic classes, religious commitments, generations, social strata, center and periphery. These deep-lying cleavages shape the political preferences of the electorate, which, in turn, shape the incentives of politicians. After all, ambitious politicians must take account of voters' views if they are to win elections. True, they often cannot respond issue by issue. But they usually can, and do, respond to the broad public mood.[2]

---

[1] Andeweg and Irwin 1993, 38.
[2] Erikson, MacKuen, and Stimson 2002.

100

This is the classic bottom-up model of politics.[3] It has two major premises: first, that voters' preferences are grounded in structural cleavages in a society and economy; and second, that politicians respond strategically to voters' preferences. There is an abundance of evidence that the first premise holds for the politics of immigration and immigrant minorities. Public opinion on issues of immigration and tolerance has been shown to be shaped by fundamental social conditions,[4] early socialization,[5] material self-interest,[6] and religious, ethnic, and national identifications.[7] There also is substantial evidence for the second premise—or, more exactly, a weak version of it.[8] On this version, politicians are entrepreneurs, on the lookout for popular concerns and resentments. They sharpen and direct them; they supply an ideological language to express them; they provide an opening for electorates to express them in political action—and thus gain political advantage for themselves. But they are agents, not principals. They respond to mass attitudes; they do not shape them.

Many of the findings of our study also are consistent with the first premise of a bottom-up model of politics. But the reality of politics makes plain that the weak version of the second premise is too weak. No one would suggest that the government of the Netherlands committed itself to a policy of multiculturalism because of pressure from below. It was quite the other way around; indeed, it generally has been the other way around for a long time. In the United States, for example, the striking feature of a policy like affirmative action has

---

[3] Lipset and Rokkan 1967 is frequently cited as a locus classicus of the bottom-up model. Important elements of their account have indeed defined the model, as it subsequently has come to be understood. However, their account is more complex, containing elements of strategic choice and top-down politics.

[4] Scheepers and his colleagues have done foundational research on attitudes toward immigrants in Western Europe. In particular, see their encyclopedic presentation of survey research on attitudes toward minorities (Coenders, Lubbers, and Scheepers 2004).

[5] Sears and Funk 1990.

[6] Quillian 1995.

[7] Huddy 2001; Fetzer 2000.

[8] See especially Kitschelt 1997 for an interweaving of electoral preferences and the entrepreneurial choices of political elites.

been precisely the continuing commitment of political elites to it in the face of its obvious and extreme unpopularity in the electorate as a whole.[9] Politics works top down as well as bottom up.[10] Politicians can be principals as well as agents; they can constrain the preferences of voters as well as respond to them.

The notion of top-down influence is not a new one, even if it is new to the politics of minorities. One of the earliest results of public opinion studies was documentation of the minimal levels of attention that ordinary citizens pay to public affairs, even during intervals (like elections) when they are paying more attention than they ordinarily are accustomed to. As long as politicians stay within this zone of inattention, they can operate relatively unconstrained by popular preferences. There was, moreover, an inertness to this inattention. Barring exceptional circumstances, what they did not know or care about today, they were not likely to know or care about tomorrow.

Research on agenda setting and issue priming has brought out a more dynamic view of top-down politics.[11] The boundaries of popular attention and awareness, it has shown, are not fixed. Issues can be made of wide concern to large numbers of the electorate. Broadly, the issues on the public agenda are those foremost in the public's mind and, what is more, at the forefront of their considerations in voting. Mass media, naturally, are the primary agents responsible for defining the public agenda and thus bringing some issues (and not others) to the attention of ordinary citizens. But leaders in politics and informed opinion, in turn, are primary agents responsible for focusing the attention of mass media on some issues rather than others. Agenda control is thus a strategic resource, as politicians actively compete to direct attention to issues that spotlight their strengths and thereby influence voters' preferences.

Agenda control is the most thoroughly studied mechanism of top-

---

[9] Sniderman and Carmines 1997.

[10] See, for example, Stokes 2000 for a more generalized exposition of the idea that bottom-up theories are "weak on agency." For a Dutch report on the findings in this chapter, see Hagendoorn and Sniderman 2004.

[11] Iyengar and Kinder 1987 is the classic study.

down politics. Here we want to investigate a less important—which is not to say unimportant—mechanism: namely, the extent to which valuing conformity renders citizens susceptible to direct pressure. Valuing conformity, we shall show, helps account for an unsuspected paradox of the politics of tolerance: the factor that propels people to respond negatively to minorities renders them susceptible to pressure to respond positively to minorities.

CULTURAL IDENTITY AND CONFORMITY

When the Dutch perceive that their culture is threatened, they react with hostility—that has been the figure in the carpet of our results. But what does it mean to believe that your national culture is threatened? What exactly is being threatened? The answer, we believe, turns on two paradoxes.

The first is this: Those who are most concerned that everyone conform to the national culture are those who are least committed to its core values. The second paradox is this: The desire for conformity is the single strongest force driving negative reactions toward minorities; yet it renders people susceptible to political and social pressures to respond positive to minorities. We start with the first paradox. But because it is more important, we concentrate on the second.

CULTURAL THREAT AND THE CULTURE OF LIBERAL DEMOCRACY

Why do people react with hostility when they fear their culture is threatened? On one level, the answer is obvious: because their culture encapsulates their understanding of what is worthy, and, therefore, worthy of defense. What is not obvious is just what they believe is being threatened.

Consider threats to economic well-being. When people are concerned about their economic prospects, they are concerned they will earn less, have less, buy less, save less; believe they are worse off than they were; and, still more, believe that they will be worse off in the future than they are now. What is the equivalent set of concerns when people are concerned about a threat to the national culture? What do they now have and value that they fear they will not have and want to avoid losing?

An initially plausible answer is the core values of their culture. What, then, are the core values of a liberal democracy like the Netherlands? You might be tempted to write a long list: promoting justice; achieving a greater measure of equality between rich and poor; preserving good traditions (acknowledging the certainty of disagreement on which ones, exactly, they are); protecting the nation against its enemies; assuring order and public safety. All, in one or another sense, are core values of a liberal democracy. But all also are politically contested. The left lays a special claim to some, without of course rejecting the others. The right lays a special claim to different ones, without of course dismissing the others.

What do the political left and right agree are core values of a liberal democracy? Two values stand out: freedom of thought and equal opportunity. The core values of liberal democracies must include these two, whatever others they may include. So we shall take commitment to freedom of thought and equal opportunity for all as a measure of commitment to the core values of the political culture of a liberal democracy.

Those who are most committed to the core values of liberal democracy should be those who are the most likely to be concerned about them. Perceiving a threat to the national culture and being committed to its core values indeed do go together—the Pearson correlation between the two is −.35—but as the sign of the coefficient indicates, the relationship is negative, not positive. Here, then, is the first paradox—those who are most concerned about preserving the national culture are the least committed to its core values.

But if it is not the core values they believe are threatened, what is it that they fear is threatened? Our hypothesis is that they fear that the rules that bind their culture together are losing their force. People no longer can be counted on to act as they should, to respect what used to command respect. The natural trust one used to have in others has been eroded, or so they feel. How can you trust someone when you can't be confident of how they will act; that they will follow the accepted rules; that they will respect the conventions of the society? In short, what lies behind a fear that their culture is being threatened is a fear that people are no longer willing to conform to established rules and standards.

It would be very easy to show that being concerned that the national culture is threatened goes along with valuing conformity. It also would prove very little. It would be just as easy to show being concerned that the national culture is being threatened goes along with being committed to authoritarian values—or, for that matter, a lack of education: both factors are correlated with valuing conformity and perceiving a threat to the national culture. We shall therefore set the bar higher. Our hypothesis is that valuing conformity is the pivotal factor immediately underlying a readiness to perceive a threat to the national culture. Figure 5.1 first shows the probability of perceiving a threat to the national culture as a function of valuing conformity,[12] controlling for authoritarianism[13] and level of formal schooling.[14]

Figure 5.1 shows that authoritarian values go along with perceiving the national culture to be threatened—just as one would expect. So,

---

[12] The degree of importance that people attach to conformity as a social value is measured with a three-item index—agreement with the idea that rules are there to be followed and people should not try to change them; that one has to be careful with people who behave differently than most people; and that those who come to live in the Netherlands should behave like the Dutch as much as possible. The conformity index has been used in a number of our studies, notably in analyses of anti-Semitism in Quebec (Sniderman et al. 1993) and hostility to immigrants in Italy (Sniderman et al. 2000). The only point of difference in the Netherlands study is the addition of the third item.

[13] Support for authoritarian values also is measured with a three-item index: agreement with the idea that it's more important to live in an orderly society in which laws are vigorously enforced than to give people too much freedom; that only the elderly, children, and handicapped should receive public assistance; and that if workers have to be fired, the first to be let go should be women with working husbands. See Sniderman et al. 2000. For stylistic variety, commitment to authoritarian values and authoritarianism are used interchangeably.

[14] Education is measured in terms of the highest school diploma obtained from elementary school through a variety of forms of high school through higher vocational school and university.

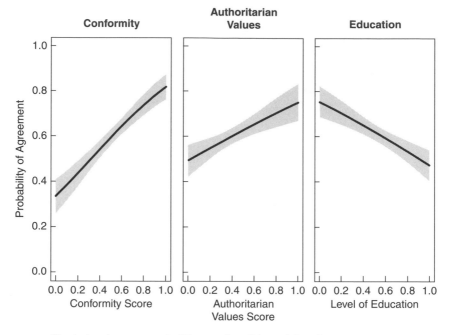

Shaded region represents 95 percent confidence interval

Probit Coefficients:
Conformity: 1.3; SE: .19, p<.001
Authoritarian: . 70, SE: . .20, p< .001
Education: -.76, SE: .18, p<.001
(N= 927)

Fig. 5.1. Sources of perceived threats to cultural identity

too, does a lack of education—also one just would expect. However, the importance people attach to the value of conformity is easily the strongest predictor of perceived threat to the national culture.[15] We have no appetite for invidious comparisons, causal or otherwise. Analysis should not be a matter of demonstrating that "my" explanatory variable is bigger than "yours." Valuing conformity may reasonably be viewed as a consequence of commitment to authoritarian val-

[15] It is worth noting that this result does not hinge on the item in the conformity index that has a direct reference to immigrants. The correlation between conformity and cultural threat perception with this item included is .44; with it excluded, .43.

ues and a lack of education,[16] in which case both matter twice over: once as causes in their own right of perceiving a threat to cultural identity, and once more as causes of conformity. For our purposes, however, the pertinent point is that, whatever the reason one comes to value conformity, valuing it is the primary pivotal factor accounting for why some are very concerned that their cultural identity is threatened while others are not concerned all.

APPEALS TO AUTHORITY AND POLITICAL EXTREMISM

Why does it matter that a desire for conformity underpins a concern for national culture and identity? Because, we will suggest, the more importance that people attach to conformity as a value, the more susceptible they are to appeals to authority.

By and large, custom and the force of law restrain citizens from taking extreme actions. They are not similarly restrained, however, from supporting extremist policies. The most effective restraint has been a refusal of mainstream parties and leaders to give them the option of extremist policies to back. The question that we want to investigate, accordingly, is how much support could be generated for extremist policies if a politician attempted to mobilize support for a policy beyond the pale.

No one doubts that public support can be mobilized for policies to require immigrants to take mandatory language instruction, for example, or indeed to restrict immigration. But these policy proposals are part of the contemporary public debate. They are legitimate questions open for public discussion. A quite different question is whether public support can be garnered for a policy beyond the pale—for example, the establishment of a legally segregated school system; that is, a school system in which Dutch children and the children of ethnic minorities would be officially separated from each other and forbidden as a matter of law from sitting next to each other in the same classrooms. Politics is the domain distinctively concerned with public

---

[16] This is the causal ordering of the "two flavors" model. See Sniderman et al. 2000.

authority. How much support can be won for a policy beyond the pale by appealing to authority?

In the baseline condition of the segregation experiment, the interviewer begins by saying, "Sometimes one hears that ethnic minority children need more attention at school than Dutch children," then the interviewer asks whether they agree or disagree "that separate schools for ethnic minority children should be established." The introduction of the question carries the suggestion that Dutch children are disadvantaged when minority children are in their classroom. It is only a suggestion, not a justification. Still, it may prime a respondent to consider the possibility that Dutch children are disadvantaged by having minority classmates. That is regrettable but unavoidable: there had to be some reason for asking such an extraordinary question. It is all the more worth noting that to the extent that the introduction does operate as a justification, it works against, not for, our experimental manipulation eliciting a significant effect.

The experimental variation begins with an appeal to science: "Scientific research shows that ethnic minority children need more attention at school than Dutch children. This may disadvantage Dutch children." Then the interviewer makes an appeal to political authority: "[T]he Ministry of Education would design a careful plan to establish separate schools for ethnic minority children." The treatment thus involves a combination of appeals, appropriately we believe. Political leaders take advantage of every means at their disposal to succeed. They do not confine themselves to just one argument, even if they think it is the single best argument. They make use of every one they think will do them some good. Hence our decision to make use of a combination of appeals: to science, to careful planning, and to the responsibility of government for the success of the school system.

The first question to consider, though not the one of most interest to us, is to explore whether an appeal to authority, in and of itself, boosts support for an extremist policy. In the baseline condition, 5 percent believe that segregation is a very good idea, and 14 percent that it is either a somewhat good idea or a very good one. By contrast, when an appeal is made to authority, 11 percent believe it is a very good idea and 24 percent that it is either a somewhat good idea or a very good one.[17] The difference between baseline and treatment conditions easily meets standard levels of statistical significance. It also, in our view, more than meets standard levels of substantive significance. There is a school system for Muslims in the Netherlands, but it is a voluntary system. Minority children may attend if they wish; more relevantly, they need not attend if they do not wish to attend. What is on the table here is quite different. Minority children would be legally prohibited from going to school with Dutch children. What is being proposed is no less than to establish an apartheid educational system in the Netherlands. We are struck by the fact that a quarter of the general public can be brought to support an officially segregated school system by an appeal to authority. But whether the impact of the appeal to authority should be seen as a large or small one we leave to the reader to judge.

The question of fundamental concern to us is: What renders some people susceptible to appeals to authority? We believe that it is valuing conformity, and the reason that it is important to test whether this is so is because conformity offers an understanding of what we believe to be a central paradox of the politics of minorities: the same factor that propels people to respond negatively to minorities renders them susceptible to pressure to respond positively to them.

Table 5.1 lays out responses when an appeal to authority is made depending on how much importance a person attaches to the value of conformity. For convenience the conformity index has been divided into (approximately) arithmetic thirds. Look first at those who attach comparatively little importance. Making an appeal to authority has no impact on them. In the baseline condition, roughly one in ten support segregated schools; in the test condition, the percentage is virtually identical. Now, look at what happens as people attach comparatively more importance to the value of conformity. For one thing, the more importance they attach to it, the more likely they are to support a proposal to establish a legally segregated school system. This is true in both the control and treatment conditions, and it is as we should expect: in our studies the value people place on conformity is the single

---

[17] Since the purpose is descriptive, the weighted sample is used.

TABLE 5.1

Percent Responding to an Appeal to Authority as a Function of the Value
of Conformity

	No Appeal (N = 964)	*Appeal (N = 1,043)*
Low conformity	8%	12%
Medium conformity	11%	24%
High conformity	20%	38%

Chi-square statistics: Low conformity = 4.96 (p = .17); Medium conformity = 30.4
(p < .01); High conformity = 20.5 (p < .01)

best predictor of their level of prejudice.[18] It is the interplay of an appeal to authority and conformity that is of interest here. As conformity increases, the potency of an appeal to authority increases, too. Even in the crude categories used in the table, the proportion of those supporting an apartheid school system approximately doubles with the treatment effect. In the control condition, 20 percent of those who attach more importance to conformity support a legally segregated school system; in the treatment condition, 38 percent do. If an appeal to authority can boost support for a policy beyond the pale, it is worth considering how effective it may be in boosting support for exclusionary policies in general.

OBSERVING HOW PEOPLE BEHAVE WHEN THEY BELIEVE THEY ARE NOT BEING INTERVIEWED

The segregation experiment carries us some distance, but it is only a beginning. Public opinion surveys only show, a familiar objection runs, how people behave in the (artificial) setting of a public opinion interview. They do not show how they behave in real life. This objection would seem to put public opinion studies in an impossible

---

[18] For example, Sniderman et al. 2000.

quandary. How is it possible to observe how people will react outside the interview situation when all we can do is to observe how they act within it?

Thinking about the social dynamics of an interview suggested a possibility to us. Well-conducted interviews promote a bond between the interviewer and the person being interviewed: familiarity increases, and a measure of rapport and trust develops. Our idea was to take advantage of this (admittedly modest) bond between interviewer and interviewee.

The intuition could not be simpler. To observe how people behave outside the interview context, tell them that the interview is over. Then, when they believe that the interview is finished, have the interviewer put pressure on them to adopt one or another position on minority issues. Specifically, in the baseline condition, the interviewer announces, "This is the final question," then asks the test item. By contrast, in the treatment condition, the interviewer—falsely—says, "The interview is finished." To reinforce the impression that the interview is over, the interviewer goes on to say, "I would like to add that I enjoyed talking to you and that your answers will be very useful to us." Of course, remarking thats she "enjoyed talking" with the respondent also pays the respondent a compliment, implying that he is an interesting and engaging person and that the interviewer feels positively toward him.

Having done her best to persuade the interviewee that the interview is over, the interviewer implicitly attempts to induce the respondent to agree with her. Specifically, she goes on to say, "Wouldn't you also agree that ethnic minorities are responsible for more social problems than is usually supposed?" The phrasing, "Wouldn't you also agree," needless to say, is intended to convey the idea that the interviewer, naturally, expects the person she has just finished interviewing to agree with her. An expectation of agreement is, in and of itself, a prime mechanism for the exercise of interpersonal influence.

The "implicit agreement" manipulation only imperfectly approximates the manipulation we wished to administer. Originally, we wanted the interviewer, after announcing the interview was over, to declare explicitly that she believed that ethnic minorities caused more social problems than is usually supposed. Also, we wanted the interviewer to say how impressed she had been by how many things the two of them agreed on. The idea was to achieve as strong a manipulation as possible. Our interviewers vetoed this. They objected to expressing anti-immigrant sentiments. They also objected to asserting that respondents' views agreed with their own when they did not. Hence our compromise of indirectness: the experimental condition is worded to create an opening for respondents to draw an inference that the interviewer shares their views and believes they share hers. No pressure is exerted to extract compliance, no sanction threatened. There is only an implied invitation to agree, extended for just an instant, "Wouldn't you also agree," though backed by a personal compliment—"I want to say that I've really enjoyed speaking with you."[19]

It was difficult to get interviewers to engage in the "end-of-the-interview" experiment, even in its watered-down form. Many discussions of the purpose of the procedure were required, and still more revisions of the wording. They agreed to participate in the experiment only when they saw it would provide a unique opportunity to observe how people being interviewed will react to a minority group when they believe they are no longer being interviewed. Even so, it is a good bet that some interviewers did not always throw themselves wholeheartedly into their roles. We regret this, but it is a comfort to know that, if there is a bias, it works against, not for, our hypothesis.

The reluctance of the interviewers nonetheless is worth bearing in mind in evaluating the results of the experimental manipulation. It has only a modest impact. In the baseline condition, 30 percent agreed that ethnic minorities were responsible for more social problems than is commonly acknowledged; in the treatment condition, 36 percent did so—a statistically significant difference but hardly a substantively impressive one. The question, though, is not whether the public as a whole can be swayed to express antiminority sentiments; it is whether

---

[19] Since this was said whether it was true or not, all respondents in the treatment condition were debriefed after the experiment. Interviewers explained that they said what they had as part of their job and then explained why they had to say what they had—in order to carry out an experiment on interpersonal influence.

TABLE 5.2

End of Interview Experiment: Percentage Agreeing Minorities Responsible
for More Problems than Commonly Acknowledged

	Agree	
	Control (N = 536)	Treatment (N = 561)
Low conformity	9%	11%
Medium conformity	31%	34%
High conformity	50%	65%

Chi-square statistics: Low conformity = .07 (p = .79); Medium conformity = .05
(p = .82); High conformity = 8.39 (p < .01)

the third of the public that values conformity is susceptible to interpersonal pressure.

Table 5.2 summarizes the proportion agreeing that minorities are
more of a problem than is commonly supposed, conditional on two
factors—whether respondents receive the experimental manipulation or not and the amount of importance they attach to conformity
as a value. The experimental treatment in the end-of-the interview
experiment has no effect on those who attach (comparatively) little
importance to conformity. In the baseline condition, only one in ten
say minorities are responsible for more problems; in the treatment
condition, the proportion doing so is identical. By contrast, the experimental treatment has a substantial effect on the third of the public
that attaches (comparatively) high importance to conformity: in the
baseline condition, one out of two declare that ethnic minorities are
responsible for more problems than is commonly supposed; in the
treatment condition, two out of three do so.[20]

The end-of-the-interview experiment and the segregation experi-

---

[20] It is also worth remarking that, whatever experimental condition they are in, the more
importance respondents attach to conformity, the more likely they are to give a negative
characterization of minorities—hardly a surprising finding in light of the fact that the value
set on conformity is the single best predictor of prejudice toward minorities.

ment are different in every operational detail—the issue at stake, the means by which pressure is exerted, and the social acceptability of anti-immigrant responses. It would be understandable if the results of the two experiments differed. In fact, they parallel each other perfectly.

A PERSPECTIVE REVERSAL

In all of our studies across a variety of countries, the single best predictor of prejudice toward minorities is the importance that people attach to the value of conformity.[21] But our hypothesis is that valuing conformity increases susceptibility to political and social pressure. This would be ironic, if true, since it would mean that the same factor that predisposes people to respond negatively to minorities also renders them susceptible to pressure to respond positively.

We anticipated this possibility. The design of the end-of-the-interview experiment has two arms. The one that we have seen tests the readiness of our respondents to agree that minorities are responsible for *more* problems than is commonly supposed. The one that we now examine tests the readiness of our respondents to agree that minorities are responsible for *fewer* problems than is commonly supposed.

Table 5.3 sets out the results. Just as one would expect, in both the control and treatment conditions, the more importance people attach to conformity, the less willing they are to respond positively to minorities. The question, though, is: Does pressure on those who value conformity inhibit their readiness to respond *negatively* to immigrants?

The first row of table 5.3 shows that interviewer pressure had no effect on those who do not value conformity. In the control condition, nine out of ten agree that immigrants cause fewer problems than is commonly supposed; in the treatment condition, again approximately nine out of ten respond positively. By contrast, among the third of the public that attaches more importance to conformity, interpersonal

---

[21] Sniderman et al. 1993, which investigated anti-Semitism in Canada; Sniderman et al. 2000, which examined intolerance toward extracommunitarians in Italy; and this study.

TABLE 5.3

End of Interview Experiment: Percentage Agreeing Minorities Responsible
for Fewer Problems than Commonly Acknowledged

	Agree	
	Control (N = 464)	*Treatment (N = 446)*
Low conformity	91%	86%
Medium conformity	73%	83%
High conformity	45%	72%

Chi-square statistics: Low conformity = 2.8 (p = .11); Medium conformity = 15.5
(p < .01); Low conformity = 15.8 (p < .01)

pressure plainly mattered. In the baseline condition, 45 percent of
those who value conformity agree that minorities are responsible for
fewer problems than is commonly supposed. In the treatment condition, however, 72 percent of them do so. Paradoxically, the single
strongest factor predisposing people to respond negatively to minorities renders them susceptible to pressure to respond positively.

Two questions immediately suggest themselves. Are those who
value conformity similarly susceptible to influence on highly charged
issues? And supposing they are, do political leaders have the capacity
to take advantage of their susceptibility to influence? To address both
questions, the party leader experiment was carried out.

THE POWER OF POLITICAL LEADERS

The principal party on the left, the Social Democrats (PvdA), has ad-
vocated and promoted multiculturalism. Some leaders of the principal party of the right, the Liberals (VVD), have defended it on the
traditional grounds of individual freedom, in this case to follow one's
own culture. But, of course, as a party of the right, multiculturalism
is at odds with the principles of the VVD as most of its members
understand them. And yet, so far from challenging the multicultural

policies of the PvdA, the VVD tacitly has acquiesced in them, to its political cost.[22]

It is not difficult to understand why the VVD—over a limited period of time—would acquiesce in a policy it opposes, even though it might benefit politically by opposing it. Public debate over minority issues, party leaders on both right and left fear, would be divisive. Open opposition to policies that assist minorities might let the genie of intolerance out of the bottle; once out, the genie might never be bottled up again. The harder problem to understand is how political leaders on the left and the right have contained opposition in the ranks of their own parties.

The hypothesis we need to test is that the same factor that predisposes people to be intolerant of minorities also renders them susceptible to respond positively to them. If true, party leaders should paradoxically be most successful in inhibiting the expression of opposition of that part of their constituency most likely to oppose policies to assist minorities.

To test this hypothesis, we carried out the party leader experiment.[23] The focus of the experiment is the principle of cultural pluralism—that is, whether Turks and Moroccans who have come to the Netherlands should be free to follow their own way of life. The VVD and PvdA are the two major political parties. Accordingly, in one condition, respondents are told that "an important VVD politician has spoken out in support of cultural pluralism"; in another, that "an important PvdA politician" has done so. Since it is only the positions of the two major parties that are manipulated, only the responses of their adherents are analyzed.

Not surprisingly, the more importance respondents attach to conformity as a value, the more strongly opposed they are to cultural pluralism. This is equally true, it is worth noting, whether they belong to

---

[22] Frits Bolkestijn is the exception that proves the rule. He vaulted the VVD forward by opposing immigration and multiculturalism.

[23] In the experiment we focus on the PvdA and the VVD, not just because they are the politically most consequential parties but because they are the only ones large enough in our sample to carry out the experimental manipulation.

TABLE 5.4
Political Leader Experiment—Mean Level of Support for Cultural Pluralism

| Conformity | VVD supporters | | PvDA supporters | |
	VVD politician	PvDA politician	VVD politician	PvDA politician
Low	0.53	0.41	0.75	0.75
Medium	0.47	0.43	0.45	0.64
High	0.46	0.15	0.14	0.47
N	104	96	100	96

Panel A F-values: Conformity = 3.8 (p < .05); VVD/PvdA experimental manipulation = 8 (p < .01).

Panel B F-values: Conformity = 42.7 (p < .001); VVD/PvdA experimental manipulation = 16.2 (p < .001).

the PvdA or the VVD.[24] The crucial question is this: Are VVD supporters who attach the most importance to conformity less likely to express opposition to cultural pluralism when their party supports it than when the PvdA does? Conversely, are PvdA supporters less like to express opposition to it when *their* party supports it?

The left panel of table 5.4 shows mean levels of support for cultural pluralism for VVD adherents conditional both on their level of conformity and whether their party or its principal opponent supports it. The right panel shows parallel results for their PvdA counterparts. Consider first responses of VVD supporters. When their opponent advocates cultural pluralism, the mean level of support of the highest third on the conformity index is .15. By contrast, when their party advocates cultural pluralism, the average level of support is .46. Just the same is true for PvdA supporters. When leaders of the other party advocate cultural pluralism, the mean level of support for cultural

---

[24] The zero-order correlation between the conformity index and opposition to cultural pluralism is .33 for the VVD and .48 for the PvdA.

pluralism among those who value conformity is .14. By contrast, when a leader of their party backs it, the mean level of support is .47.

In short, the results of the party leader experiment match those of the segregation and end-of-the-interview experiments. All show that those who prize conformity will tend to yield to political and social pressure—even when doing so means doing the opposite of what they themselves are predisposed to doing.

FOCAL POINTS

The issues most prominent in the public agenda tend to be the issues uppermost in citizens' minds as well as the ones most relevant to voters' choices. Politicians hardly have complete control over what issues are at the center of attention. What is more, electoral competition tends to generate competing interests, with each side trying to train the public spotlight on the issues that work to their benefit and keep in the background those that work to their disadvantage. But politicians do have a measure of control over which issues become a focal point and, more important in this case, which do not.

A striking feature of politics in the Netherlands, we have observed, was a cross-party consensus to keep the issue of multiculturalism off the public agenda. Not until the election of 2001 was the issue brought to the fore. The result was an electoral upheaval. The upheaval, however, coincided with a conjunction of two factors—the issue of multiculturalism being brought to the fore and the exceptional appeal of the candidate bringing it to the fore. Therefore, it is natural to ask whether the exceptional reaction was tied to the exceptional appeal of the candidate.

A policy of multiculturalism is an invitation to a politics of colliding identities—"our" way of life versus "their" way of life. But some invitations are declined. The question, then, is how easily can exclusionary reactions be provoked by bringing considerations of collective identity to the fore? But this question begs another. What does it mean to bring considerations of collective identity to the fore?

On one view, it takes a major event to make them salient. An analogue of a major event, in our world of experiments, is a major intervention like the one in the segregation experiment. There, the idea was to measure the impact of an appeal to authority on the positions people take on controversial issues. Because the policy—creating a legally segregated school system—was extreme, the strategy was to make the appeal strong, combining the authority of science and the ministry of education. Here, our strategy is just the opposite: to make the intervention weak to see if the *mere mention* of considerations of collective identity suffices to evoke exclusionary reactions.

In the national versus individual identity experiment, respondents are randomly assigned to one of three experimental conditions. In the first condition, their identity as individuals is primed. In this condition, the question begins with the introduction, "People differ in many ways and each human being is unique. One person likes music, another likes to go for a walk, still another likes to go out. Everyone is different." In the second condition, their identity as Dutch citizens is primed. In this condition, the question begins with the introduction, "People belong to different types of groups. One of the most important and essential of these groups is the nation that you belong to. In your case, you belong to the Dutch nationality. Each nation is different." In the third condition, neither their national nor their individual identity is primed. By seeing whether responses in this default condition are more similar to those in the national or personal priming conditions, we can gauge in which frame people ordinarily see themselves when being asked their views about immigrants.

In all three conditions, respondents are asked if more barriers should be raised to immigration. The political question is this: A large number feel that their national identity is important to them. But a large number do not. Is it primarily those who attach great importance who respond when national identity is brought to the fore? Or is there a wider circle of reaction? The second alternative, a wider circle of reaction, seems the better bet to us. People's national identity is important to a wide swath in a society; indeed, it is important even to those who do not think it is.

Under ordinary circumstances, it is not a consideration that comes to mind, or if it does, it is not a consideration to which they give much

weight. All the same, when the issue of national identity becomes salient in a specific situation, they react. We need, then, to take account
both of whether people's national identity is salient in a particular situation and of the importance they attach to it. If bringing national
identity to the fore matters for those for whom it is important, they
should react especially strongly when it becomes salient.

Table 5.5 shows that priming people to think of themselves as individuals (as compared to saying nothing at all) has no effect. But this is
what one would expect. Why should an exclusionary reaction be more
likely if a person's attention is directed toward himself as an individual? Still, this finding—or this absence of a finding—is telling. It indicates that people's ordinary state of mind is to think in terms of
their personal, not their national, identity—even when the issue has
to do with immigrant minorities.

All this, with the possible exception of the last, one might expect.
But what one would not expect is that the less importance people attach to their national identity, the more likely they are to react when
their national identity is primed.[25] Yes, it sounds odd to say this, but
close examination of the results clears up a first impression of oddity.
Support for making immigration more difficult is very nearly univer-
sal among those who attach great importance to their national identity. As a practical matter, there is a ceiling effect: so many of them
already are on one side of the issue that there is no room for the additional stimulus of priming their national identity to have an effect.

It is only natural to suppose that identity politics matters for those
for whom considerations of national identity matter—that is, matter
consciously. It is another thing to learn, as we do here, that it also matters for those who in ordinary circumstances do not view their national identity as important to them.

There is a fundamental dynamic here. Bringing considerations of
collective identity to the fore enlarges the coalition opposed to immigration—above and beyond those already predisposed to oppose it.
And the people who are brought into the coalition tend to be among
the most educated and have the highest occupational status. By mak-

---

[25] This is the meaning of the negative sign of the interaction term in the first equation.

TABLE 5.5

Regression of Support for Immigration Restrictions with
National and Personal Primes

	National prime	Personal prime
Prime	.34	.14
	(.20)	(.20)
Dutch ID	1.67***	1.66***
	(.24)	(.24)
Prime X Dutch ID	−.75*	−.30
	(.32)	(.33)
1st cut point	−.22	−.23
2nd cut point	.18	.20
3rd cut point	.95	.94
L-likelihood	−790	−765
N	679	670

ing issues of identity a focal point of political argument, politicians can provoke exclusionary reactions, not just among the ranks of the intolerant but in all quarters of society. It is the responsiveness of those who ordinarily do not view their national identity as important that helps explain, we believe, the "flash" potential of identity politics.

TOP-DOWN POLITICS

Our findings show that a large part of the electorate, on the order of a third, is susceptible to social and political pressures to modify their reactions to minorities. One might reply, true, but the largest part of the electorate is not. This strikes us as too sanguine a response. In a public opinion interview, one can exert only modest pressure. In real life, such pressure can come at gale force.

But there is a deeper point. The same findings that point to top-down influence also point to its limits. These limits are not the result of historical accidents. The pre–September 11 equilibrium over multiculturalism, the totality of our results suggest, was inherently unstable. Making minorities and multiculturalism the focal point of public attention and argument generated a deep-lying suspicion, a belief that Muslim immigrants wanted to live in their new country but not be a part of it; a suspicion of divided loyalty that took root not just at the periphery but at the center of society—among the most educated, best off, and most tolerant. This suspicion of divided loyalties, reinforced by the affirmation of the separateness of Muslims, coupled with the absence of their affirmation of their most fundamental loyalty to the country they had come to, was there before September 11. Sooner or later, but more likely sooner than later, a politician and a party would have brought issues of national identity to the fore, then done all in their power, perhaps out of a desire for power but possibly also out of principle, to profit from the flash potential of identity politics. Fortuyn was an exceptional individual, but his meteoric political rise was not a historical accident.

CHAPTER 6

Tolerance

PUBLIC OPINION SURVEYS cannot provide a blueprint for public policy. They can speak to principles that should guide policy, if policy is to be accepted as legitimate. Our concern, accordingly, is with principles that should guide a liberal democracy's course of action when ways of life collide. We have seen the potency of concerns about cultural identity; the persisting power of prejudice; the consequences of value conflicts; and the power of social and political pressure to evoke—or inhibit—exclusionary reactions to immigrant minorities. Here is what we have concluded from what we have observed.

IDENTITY POLITICS

Only a few years ago to criticize multiculturalism was to risk charges of racism. In Western Europe the climate of opinion has changed. Multiculturalism still has many supporters, particularly among the more politically engaged. But it now has many critics, including some of the most politically engaged. What is responsible for so profound a change?

The answer appears obvious. The post–September 11 world is very different from what preceded it. How could it not be? What had been inconceivable had become not merely conceivable but had been witnessed—seen, as it were, firsthand through images televised around the world. Yet our findings indicate that the bases for the political challenge to multiculturalism were laid before September 11, which is also to say not because of it.

Multiculturalism was launched to protect and promote the distinctive identities and ways of life of minorities. The policy assumes that minorities wish to preserve their identities and ways of life; believe that their well-being is tied to preserving them; are concerned that they are threatened; and are right in believing them to be threatened. These assumptions raise many questions, not because they are unreasonable in themselves but because they are complex and can frame questions in ways that invite some answers and discourage others. Our findings throw light on answers to only some questions, although they also suggest how some others may be framed better. We begin with the question of a threat to ways of life.

The premise of multiculturalism is a belief that the ways of life of minorities, especially those of Muslims, need and deserve government support and official recognition. The underlying impulse is sympathetic, generous; sensitive to the difficulties of becoming a member of a new society; intent on offering a helping hand. It is all the more ironic that its sensitivity to the threats that immigrant minorities perceive to their way of life has been accompanied by an insensitivity to the threats that the majority perceive to *their* way of life.

Myopia is understandable; in hindsight, even perhaps unavoidable. The majority, it seems obvious, can take care of themselves—they are in control, after all. But, purely as a matter of fact, large numbers of them perceive that *their* way of life is now threatened, and whether their concern is in the end justifiable, it is not unreasonable.

Cultural diversity is hardly a new fact in Western Europe. But a common history is not necessarily the same as a shared history, and the history of all the Western European countries is a history of "us" versus "them" within each country. The Netherlands is an apt example, since the principle of separate Protestant, Catholic, and non-confessional communities only lost force in the last generation. Nonetheless, the scale and speed with which Western Europe now is becoming culturally diverse is unprecedented. And the collision of ideas of right and wrong involves points of difference that genuinely matter to people on both sides—points of difference, moreover, that are visible and with the surge in the number of Muslims in the Netherlands are becoming still more so.

Nor is it just the facts on the ground. There is also the power of multiculturalism both as policy and symbol. The whole point of the policy, after all, is to change the values and institutions of the society—to create a society in which majority and minority cultures are more nearly equal in standing. What is more, this process of change is—or at any rate is publicly presented as—a process of mutual negotiation—the majority community on one side of the table, the Muslim community on the other. Indeed, a proposal of the European Commission at one point went so far as to characterize "migrants as 'partners' of receiving states."[1] The public does not know the phrases of formal documents, but they can pick up the drift of things all the same. Hence the irony: the more credible the commitment of the government to allay the concern of Muslim minorities that their ways of life are threatened, the more reasonable the concern of the majority community that *its* values are threatened.

Of course, because change is on the agenda, it does not follow that those who say they fear change object out of a fear of change. They may have quite different concerns—for example, that their standard of living will suffer. They are not necessarily dissembling when they say they perceive a threat to their cultural identity, though no doubt some are. But whether they recognize it or not, their root concern is about their economic well-being, not their cultural identity.

And so it is for some, as we have seen. Economic self-interest underpins cultural threat. True, self-interest has never been the dominating force in any of our analyses. But it would be a bit hasty to conclude that self-interest cannot be a powerful driver of hostility to minorities. If anything, we would draw the opposite conclusion. If concerns about economic well-being have a substantial impact, both in their own right and as a source of cultural threat, in prosperous times, one can only imagine their impact in hard times.

In the present circumstances, the concern about cultural identity is the dominant factor. It can hardly come as a surprise that those who are most concerned that the national culture is threatened are also those who attach the most importance to their national identity. If this

---

[1] Joppke 2005, 237.

does not qualify as a tautology, it certainly makes the grade as a truism, which makes it all the more curious that political leaders have acted as though it is false. It takes no power of insight to know that a lot of people care a lot about issues of national identity, or that they are likely to react negatively rather than positively if its status is called into question. It does not follow that public leaders should do less than they can to find a basis that minority and majority can come to accept as legitimate; still less that they cannot succeed at finding such a basis. It does follow that it is a risky business to make differences in ways of life a focal point of public attention and political argument.

We had anticipated this. What we had not anticipated, as obvious as it now seems, is that issues of identity come into play in a second, politically more significant way. The analogy in our minds at the start was to lighting a fire: the drier the wood, the easier it is to ignite. So the greater people's concerns about threats to the national culture, the easier they are, as it were, to ignite politically. This analogy, if apt, has implications for politics. The constituency for identity politics, it implies, is not easily expansible. Political leaders have the power to excite a reaction from those already concerned about the issue of national identity; they do not have the power to break out of this constituency and win strong support from those who do not think there is any threat to the Dutch way of life.

In a set of experiments, we saw that making considerations of national identity momentarily *salient* evokes as strong a reaction from those who *strongly disagree* that the Dutch way of life is threatened as from those who are the most concerned that it is. It cannot come as a surprise to observe that issues of identity matter for those who say they are important. It should come as a surprise that they matter as much for those who say they are not important. There are gains to be had by bringing to the fore differences in ways of life that otherwise cannot be had. But there also are costs. Focusing attention on national identity leads a substantial number of people who otherwise would support inclusionary policies to support exclusionary ones. It is one thing to fail to win support you were unlikely to get; quite another to lose support you otherwise would have had.

Yet it is only natural to wonder whether what people say and do in a public opinion interview approximates what they say and do in real life. There are, after all, pressures on the person being interviewed to respond as he believes the interviewer wishes him to respond. But in gauging the validity of our experiments, the issue of interviewer pressure cuts just the opposite way. Their results are more credible because the pressures are weak, not strong. We have, for example, sprinkled pages with accounts of the impact of hypothetical "threats" to national identity or economic well-being. But this is hyperbole. No one is threatened. In one experiment, for example, immigrants are described as not "speak[ing] Dutch fluently," or the other way around. This "threat" manipulation does not bear comparison with a real life threat. It nonetheless substantially boosts opposition to immigration. Hence the paradoxical conclusion: the results of the experiments are telling just because the experimental manipulations are modest. If even modest manipulations can increase opposition to immigrants and immigration, imagine the power of real life events to do so.

Identity politics is not the only, or even necessarily the primary, force driving issues involving immigrant minorities. Informed observers and political leaders have stressed—indeed, more or less concentrated on—the impact of prejudice in generating opposition to policies to assist immigrants. It is all the more puzzling, given their stress on prejudice, that so little is known about it. There have been many first-class studies of the presumed consequences of prejudice in Western Europe[2] but hardly any of prejudice itself. The force most regard as the most important ironically is the one that has been least studied.

In the absence of research, a mythology has taken root. Overt prejudice, many social scientists have come to believe, has lost its hold, or at a minimum is ashamed to show its face in public.[3] Would that it were so. Our results show that intolerance is abundant and in plain sight. Never less than a fifth, and often a third or more, describe

---

[2] Social science in Western Europe has built up an impressive archive of studies of public opinion on issues of immigration and immigrant minorities (see especially Coenders, Lubbers, and Scheepers 2004). This has had the unfortunate effect, in the minds of some, of equating intolerance and, say, criticism of multiculturalism. The two are strongly connected but by no means the same thing.

[3] Dovidio, Glick, and Rudman 2005.

immigrant minorities as "lazy . . . complainers . . . intrusive . . . dishonest . . . violent . . . not law-abiding . . . selfish." A smaller but significant number run through a litany of complaints. What is more, their complaints are blind in a fundamental sense. As the switch experiment demonstrated, you cannot tell when those who are consistently negative have stopped talking about one minority and started talking about another.

The Netherlands is celebrated for its tolerance. Italy does not have the same reputation for tolerance, but neither does it have one for intolerance. The Netherlands' reputation, our results have shown, is deserved in one sense and undeserved in another. On the one hand, the proportion of the public that expresses no negative judgments about immigrant minorities is twice as large as it is in Italy. On the other hand, the proportion intolerant is substantially the same in both. Curiously, the Netherlands is both more tolerant than, and as intolerant as, Italy. National honors for tolerance aside, the more important question is how much power intolerance has to shape the political positions of the public at large. Yardsticks are useful. Decades of research have shown that authoritarianism is a powerful driver of antiminority reactions; less research has shown political extremism to do so as well, primarily because there has been less research. Prejudice, however, has a far more powerful impact than either authoritarian or antidemocratic values on support for the most fundamental form of equality in a liberal democracy—equal rights.

A CONFLICT OF VALUES

Together with nearly everybody else, we have been struck by the collision between Western European and Muslim values. On some points, they have not merely different but diametrically opposing convictions: what Western Europeans believe is right, Muslims believe is wrong; what Muslims believe is right, Western Europeans believe is wrong. How does one show respect for women? What are their rights? What should their status be compared to that of men? How should parents raise their children? What are the obligations of parents to children? Of children to parents?

There is deep disagreement over answers to these questions. From a Western European perspective, Muslim men dominate Muslim women. They do not have the same freedom as Muslim men to live the lives they wish to live—to pursue the career of their choosing; to go out when and with whom they wish; to be equal in status with their husband within the family. Again from a Western European perspective, Muslim children are brought up in an authoritarian, punitive, insular way. By contrast, from a Muslim perspective, Western European women are not given the respect that they deserve; their embodiment of the family honor is not acknowledged; the dangers of sexual freedom are not taken into account. Again from a Muslim perspective, Western European children are not given the discipline they need. Two ideas of what is right and what is wrong—two ideas that are not only different but in conflict.

The terms of this conflict, not just the fact of conflict, matter. Some observers believe that the clash is one of religious worldviews. "Islam has emerged as the focus of immigration debates in Europe," Zolberg and Woon write, because European identity, despite national variations, remains deeply embedded in Christian tradition, in relation to which Muslim immigrants constitute a visible "other."[4] This view seems to us right about Muslims, wrong about the "Christian majority." Religion is integral to Muslims' conception of governance. A "Muslim society" is not primarily a society of Muslims. It is a society where God-given law *makes people Muslims*.[5] Just the reverse is true for the "Christian majority." The separation of God-given and secular law is integral to their conception of governance.

There is thus a sharp division between Western European and Muslim ways of life, which is by no means to say a fixed one. The Dutch experience is a textbook example of the quicksilver character of cultures. It has become a cliché that tolerance expansively understood—encompassing full equality for women, gay rights, acceptance of drugs, and sexual freedom broadly interpreted, among other elements—is a distinctively Dutch value. But it was very nearly the other way around

[4] Zolberg and Woon 1999.
[5] We owe this formulation to Professor Jean Leca.

only a (historically) short time ago. Even after World War II, the Netherlands was characterized by traditional male-female roles; gender segregation in primary schools and in the church on Sundays; fear of nudity and sexuality; physical punishment of children; an ideology of family solidarity over individualism; and immense respect for authority. Paradoxically, the values now taken to be distinctively Dutch clash with traditionally Dutch values.

Still, for extended stretches of time, core values of a culture encapsulate people's convictions about what they are obliged to do and what they are prohibited from doing. So it seemed obvious to us that a clash of values between Western Europeans and Muslim immigrants must drive a wedge between them. Broadly, the severity of a conflict of values between the two should be proportional to the importance of a value and the ease of observing its violation. If this reasoning is right, the clash between Muslim and Western European values should be severe. The dispute is not about abstract normative principles. It is about matters of genuine importance, to real people, that can readily be observed in everyday life. You cannot miss seeing restrictions on Muslim women or the absence of them for Dutch women; the "authoritarian" manner of Muslim childrearing, the "permissive" one of Dutch.

Dutch governments have made a broad commitment to preserving, indeed, promoting, a Muslim way of life—or more exactly, one version of a Muslim way of life. Other less puritanical, though no less religious, versions of Islam have been set to one side.[6] The state instead has concentrated its efforts on preserving and promoting a particular version of Muslim practices and institutions—one that holds sway in rural and remote areas. The commitment of the government to multiculturalism was a good-faith commitment. No one anticipated that liberal values would be used to legitimize illiberal practices. But so they have. What other reaction could the majority have but to reject Muslim immigrants? What other conclusion could they draw but to oppose cultural pluralism and to press for assimilation?

A large segment of Dutch society takes strong exception to Muslim treatment of women, although not to Muslims themselves. Actually,

[6] See El fadl 2002.

to say that they do not take exception to Muslims understates what they think and feel. They have a positive regard for them. They agree that Muslims have a lot to offer Dutch culture; they believe that Muslims respect other cultures; and they reject the idea that Western European and Muslim ways of life cannot be reconciled. We had not foreseen this—that many could have a strongly negative view of Muslim values, yet a strongly positive view of Muslims themselves. And, to be candid, when we saw that they *said* this is what they thought, we did not take them at their word. Instead, we searched for every way possible to show that they were only paying lip service to norms of politeness. We came across many pieces of evidence of sincerity. But the turning point was when we examined a covert measure of prejudice, the list experiment, when our respondents thought they could say anything they wanted about minorities without anybody being aware of it. Yet again, their response was as positive as those who have positive attitudes toward Muslims *and* Muslim treatment of women and children.

Even then, we surmised that thinking well of Muslims was as far as they could go. For the longest time, it did not occur to us that they nonetheless would support the right of Muslims to follow their way of life in the Netherlands, even though they believed that it was morally wrong. In fact, they do.

Even now, looking at this result from a literal perspective, it appears to us a contradiction. Doesn't it amount to saying you are committed to liberal values, yet you are willing to accept illiberal practices? But that is the point. They are willing to accept some illiberal practices just because they are committed to liberal values, above all, tolerance. They do not grudgingly accept Muslim immigrants. They think well of them and wish them well. And because they are well disposed to them, a conflict between the values of the two groups does not aggravate conflict between them.

There is a broader point. The standard image of supporters of anti-immigration parties is of "low educated angry white men," to borrow a characterization of van der Brug, a Dutch political scientist.[7]

---

[7] Van der Brug 2003.

The impetus for the emergence of radical anti-immigrant parties, on this view, comes from the "losers of modernity": the older; the poorer; the religious; the poorly educated; the blue-collar workers threatened by low-wage immigrants; and, more expansively, all threatened by change in postindustrial societies.[8] The political battle over issues of minorities is between those at the center of liberal democracies and those at their periphery.

Perversely, just because this characterization is so obviously true, it has obscured a larger truth. Discontent at the periphery obscured its emergence at the center of liberal democracies. The basis for a new cleavage—not instead of the one between center and periphery but in addition to it, running through the center itself—was laid down in the very years when the consensus for multiculturalism appeared unshakable.[9] Then, when Fortuyn stepped forward as a critic of multiculturalism, there was a political eruption. It was not a product of Fortuyn's exceptional appeal; his meteoric rise was a product of it. Hence the mistake of equating Fortuyn with Le Pen or Haider. Fortuyn was the first to fuse appeals to national identity and the values of liberal democracy. With this cartwheel, he captured the moral high ground. Fortuyn defended the right of Muslims to express intolerance. But he claimed the right to say they were intolerant. It was wrong to deny women equality and to exploit them sexually. It was wrong to vilify gays and to call for a campaign against them. The Dutch culture was one of tolerance and equality, and it deserved to be defended. Fortuyn was the first to turn the moral tables in the argument over multiculturalism. He will not be the last.

"MERE" TOLERANCE AND MULTICULTURALISM

The Netherlands, all agree, has been "an exemplary case of immigrant multiculturalism."[10] It has awarded special influence to minority com-

---

[8] Ibid.

[9] For evidence on the continuity of political attitudes between 1998, the time of our survey, and 2002, see Van Holsteyn, Irwin, and den Ridder 2003.

[10] Phalet and Orkeny 2001, 16. For more detail, see Vermeulen and Penninx 2001.

munity leaders; established a separate state-funded school system for minorities; funded and organized housing projects designed to accommodate their religious practices; dedicated a significant portion of public radio and television media broadcasting time to minority interests; and in a variety of ways increased the power of spokesmen for the Muslim community who pride themselves on rejecting Western European values. But if the degree of its commitment to multiculturalism in the Netherlands is exceptional, the reasoning underlying it is typical.

It is necessary to go beyond mere tolerance, the argument runs.[11] This claim has been the single sharpest spur to multiculturalism and would be easier to understand if tolerance were defined modestly. In fact, it is defined expansively. "Mere" tolerance is standardly understood to mean freedom for groups to develop and defend their identity and values "in private or through associations of their members"; public assistance targeted to minorities to help them make educational and economic advances; and what is more, an injunction on government to respect the cultural identity of minorities.[12] Why is it necessary to go further than tolerance—even tolerance expansively defined?

The root reason, proponents of multiculturalism contend, is that tolerance merely requires that the larger society *puts up* with minorities. Their acceptance on its face is grudging and patronizing, it is said. Toleration suggests an act of generosity "from those who have the power to interfere but refrain from doing so . . . it is the tolerant who come out covered in glory. The tolerated, meanwhile, end up with what many of them will feel as a poor second best, for toleration is a poor substitute for recognition."[13] To settle for tolerance concedes the validity of the larger society's disapproval of minority practices and values. Hence the necessity to go beyond mere tolerance to ensure minorities have the recognition and affirmation that they both deserve and need.

In a political context, it is natural to think of tolerance as a willing-

[11] Parekh 2000.
[12] Miller 1999, 63.
[13] Philips 1999.

ness "to put up with" ideas or people you dislike. To support the right of people you agree with is no proof of tolerance. You must be ready to support the right of those you disagree with, even those you intensely dislike and disagree with. But political tolerance is one thing; social tolerance quite another. It makes no sense to say you must dislike a minority to be tolerant of it. Disagreement or dislike is not a necessary condition of social tolerance. Otherwise one would have to be bigoted in order to have a possibility of being tolerant.

There is a continuum of feelings toward minorities. The intolerant dislike, belittle, and ill treat minorities; the tolerant like, think well of, and are well disposed toward them. Advocates of multiculturalism have spotlighted the former but ignored the latter. To be truly tolerant it is not enough to be willing to "put up" with minorities; one must be well disposed toward them.

Social tolerance has more power than people recognize, indeed, more power than we had recognized. It can overcome even deep disagreements about right and wrong. Western European and Muslim ways of life do collide at some points. Each believes that what the other believes is right, is wrong; indeed, an affront to how decent people should live. Yet those who strongly disagree with traditional Muslim practices but think well of Muslims themselves—a substantial portion of the Dutch public—are genuinely well disposed toward Muslims. They are as supportive of the right of Muslims to follow their own way of life in the Netherlands as their fellow citizens whose attitudes toward Muslims are positive in every respect.

This commitment to tolerance, although broad, is not without limits. Moreover, tolerance is not the only issue of importance. Immigrants' success in education, jobs, and opportunities in their new country are issues of fundamental importance. For that matter, tolerance does not automatically translate into a political position. One person can believe that the government should do more to help minorities; another that they should do less; yet both can be equally tolerant.

Still, the benefits of tolerance are large and the costs negligible. By contrast, the material benefits of multiculturalism appear negligible and the costs high. Relative to native Dutch, immigrant minorities are worse off in the Netherlands—more likely to be unemployed, less likely to finish intermediate schooling, poorer than their fellow citi-zens—than immigrant minorities in other major Western European countries.[14] Moreover, the whole thrust of multiculturalism is to ac-centuate, even exaggerate, differences between majority and minority and insist on their importance. "Our" way of life versus "theirs"; "our" language versus "theirs"; "our" religion (or lack of it) versus "theirs"; "our" ideas of fairness and respect versus "theirs"; and "our" values versus "theirs." One consequence of this accentuation of differences is opposition to policies to help minorities—opposition piled on top of the opposition grounded in prejudice. Another conse-quence is hostility to minorities—hostility piled on top of the hostil-ity rooted in prejudice. Sharing a common identity builds support for inclusion; bringing differences of ethnic and religious identity to the fore evokes the very exclusionary reactions it is meant to avoid.[15]

DEGREES OF FREEDOM

Our findings do not speak to what will happen, but they do make plain that what has happened was not foreordained.

It is widely assumed that citizens know where they are on issues in-volving minorities and care deeply about what is done. Political lead-ers, in consequence, have to respond to their constituents' views or risk defeat. Hence the need to identify the deeper-lying forces—occu-pation, education, religion, and age most prominently among them—that shape citizens' attitudes toward immigrant issues.

This bottom-up model of politics holds for many domains of pol-icy and, in a long enough run, perhaps for all. It is natural to think that electoral politics usually operate this way. Yet the government of the Netherlands did not commit itself to multiculturalism because of elec-toral pressures from the majority. Politicians followed the advice of policy advisors and leaders of informed opinion, not public opinion,

[14] See Koopmans 2005.

[15] For evidence of the integrative effect of a common or "superordinate" identity, see Gaertner and Dovidio 2000.

when they committed themselves to a policy of multiculturalism. And they did not persist in it because they imagined that it had broad electoral appeal. They did what they did because they thought they had good reason to do it—because they had to respond to practical problems and because they wished to put the power of government to humane use. In a word, the politics of multiculturalism has operated top down, not bottom up.

Politicians have kept multiculturalism in place for so long through their control of the public agenda. Mainstream parties of the left and right agreed not to contest it. Voters cannot express opposition to multiculturalism if no candidate opposes it. Politicians have some freedom to maneuver because political representation is a blunt instrument: it does not operate issue by issue. They also can shape the electorate's preferences. Two of our experiments, the end-of-the-interview experiment and the party leader experiment, focused on the degree to which the positions that ordinary citizens take can be influenced even on hot-button issues. Both teach the same lesson. To the extent that they have committed themselves to conformity as a value, citizens can be pressured to support a policy they otherwise would oppose, and oppose a policy they otherwise would support.

The lesson is a curious one. In every political party, there is a faction especially ready to respond negatively to minorities. Paradoxically, it is the one that most easily can be influenced to respond positively to them. They can most easily be influenced because they attach the most importance to the value of conformity; and the more importance people attach to conformity, the more susceptible to influence they are. Hence the paradox: those who are most likely to respond negatively to immigrant minorities are most susceptible to influence to respond positively to them. Ironically, the intolerant afford politicians an extra margin to maneuver in favor of tolerance.

Having the power to influence the views of citizens is one thing; how it is put to use is quite another. Political and intellectual leaders in Western Europe have taken the tack that those who question multiculturalism do so out of prejudice. It has followed that they should be shamed out of their opposition if possible, ignored if not. The explosion of popular support for Fortuyn when he criticized multiculturalism suggests that the strategy of shaming or ignoring was a costly mistake. The political and intellectual elite could never have won the support of the intolerant. They did not need to lose the support of the tolerant. They made them their opponents because they did not feel a need to make them their supporters.

As things stand now, liberal democracy is not at risk from extreme anti-immigrant parties on the right.[16] Political and social elites in Western Europe also remain supportive of inclusion for reasons of prudence as well as principle. Then, too, the segment of the public broadly sympathetic to immigrant minorities is substantially larger than the segment that is hostile. The question is not whether government should assist and protect minorities, but rather what principles should guide its efforts.

Our work points to two. The first is loyalty. Only one negative judgment distinguishes Muslim minorities from other minorities. They are twice as likely to be judged as more loyal to their own country and government than to Dutch society. It is not just the comparative frequency with which they are characterized as disloyal that is worth remarking. It also is the absolute frequency. Nearly one out of every two Dutch believe that Muslim immigrants pledge their loyalty to their old country, not to their new one. Moreover, suspicions of disloyalty show up in all quarters of society, including the most tolerant. Remember the reactions of the large segment of Dutch society whose evaluation of Muslim treatment of women and children is negative yet whose evaluation of Muslims themselves is positive. On the one hand, they are as fully supportive of Muslims' right to follow their own way of life in the Netherlands as those whose evaluation of both Muslims and Muslim practices is positive. On the other hand, they are just as likely as the average citizen to believe that Muslims maintain their loyalty to their old country and withhold from their new one.

This suspicion of disloyalty has a basis in reality. Many Muslim immigrants wish to live in liberal societies but not be part of them. They believe that they ought not to be bound by the ground rules of a liberal democracy when they conflict with their religious tenets. In the

[16] Joppke 2005.

name of multiculturalism, for example, Muslim community leaders claim that Islamic sharia law should prevail in civil cases related to the Muslim community. Multiculturalism has helped to make it unclear whether Muslim immigrants as a community will commit themselves to a liberal society like the Netherlands, because it has made it unclear whether they should. On the one hand, multiculturalism gives incentives to leaders of Muslims communities to emphasize the disjunction between themselves and the majority culture. On the other hand, it gives more reasons to the majority to believe that there is indeed a disjunction. In both ways, multiculturalism lends credibility to an image of Muslim immigrants living in their new country yet living, as it were, outside it. The issue of a common identity and shared loyalty that minority and majority share is a fundamental one. A pledge of loyalty to the larger society is the basis for, not the antithesis, of diversity. More the pity, then, that the issue of loyalty was not addressed before September 11, making it all the more difficult to lay it to rest afterward.

The second principle is tolerance—tolerance understood to encompass not merely putting up with minorities but also being well disposed toward them. Putting a spotlight on tolerance both defines how people *should* act toward those who are different and motivates them *in fact to act* as they should act. Tolerance thus contributes twice over to a society that is diverse and values diversity. By contrast, focusing a spotlight on differences in collective identities undercuts support for both diversity and tolerance.

There is a final irony. The aim of multiculturalism is conciliation. But so far as it brings issues of cultural identity to the fore, it increases the hostility of the majority to Muslim minorities. And so far as it strengthens traditional institutions, it increases the hostility of Muslim minorities to the majority and, what is more, to other minorities. As we write, headlines in Western Europe report assassinations and death threats, the burning of mosques and churches, and attacks on Jews and Jewish property.[17] There is more than one lesson to learn, but the most important is that "mere" tolerance has been a badly underrated virtue.

[17] Schoenfeld 2004.

OUR STUDY IS BASED on a wide-ranging survey of the prejudices and values of Dutch citizens. The survey research facility at the University of Utrecht carried out a national survey from January to April 1998. The sample was collected by randomly selecting telephone numbers; the person to be interviewed was randomly selected from each household. In all, 2,007 interviews of adult Dutch (age sixteen and older) were carried out. We want to call attention to the response rate: 37 percent. Response rates are dropping for public opinion surveys, but this is nonetheless on the low side. The interview was approximately forty-five minutes long and took advantage of computer-assisted interviewing, allowing us to combine the advantages of randomized experiments and large-scale survey research. It is these experiments that enable us to catch sight of phenomena that, until now, have been hidden from view. Data and the codebook are available through the Data Archive of the Survey Research Center of the University of California, Berkeley.

Ali, A. Hirsi 2002. *De zoontjesfabriek: Over vrouwen, islam en integratie* (The factory producing sons: About women, Islam, and integration). Amsterdam: Augustus.

Allport, G. 1988. *The Nature of Prejudice.* Reading, MA: Addison-Wesley.

Andeweg, R., and G. Irwin. 1993. *Dutch Government and Politics.* Houndmills: Macmillan.

———. 2003. *Governance and Politics in the Netherlands.* London: Palgrave MacMillan.

Arends-Tóth, J., and F. Van De Vijver. 2003. "Multiculturalism and Acculturation: Views of Dutch and Turkish-Dutch." *European Journal of Social Psychology* 33: 249–66.

Banaji, M., B. Nosek, and A. Greewald. 2004. "No Place for Nostalgia in Science." *Psychological Inquiry* 15:279–310.

Benhabib, S. 2002a. *The Claims of Culture.* Princeton: Princeton University Press.

———. 2002b. In "'Nous' et 'les Autres': The Politics of Complex Cultural Dialogue in a Global Civilization." In C. Joppke and S. Lukes, eds., *Multicultural Questions.* Oxford: Oxford University Press.

Blalock, H. 1967. *Toward a Theory of Minority Group Relations.* New York: John Wiley.

Blumer, H. 1958. "Race Prejudice as a Sense of Group Position." *Pacific Sociological Review* 1:3–7.

Bobo, L. 1983. "Whites' Opposition to Busing: Symbolic Racism or Realistic Group Conflict?" *Journal of Personality and Social Psychology* 45:1196–1210.

———. 1999. "Prejudice as Group Position: Microfoundations of a Sociological Approach to Racism and Race Relations." *Journal of Social Issues* 55:445–72.

———. 2001. "Racial Attitudes and Relations at the Close of the Twentieth Century." In N. Smelser, W.J. Wilson, and F. Mitchell, eds., *America Becoming: Racial Trends and Their Consequences.* Washington, DC: National Academy Press.

Bobo, L., and E. Garcia. 1992. "The Chippewa Indian Treat Rights Survey." Working Paper No. 9. Robert M. La Follette Institute of Public Affairs, University of Wisconsin–Madison.

Bobo, L., and V. Hutchings. 1996. "Perceptions of Racial Group Competition: Extending Blumer's Theory of Group Position to a Multiracial Social Context." *American Sociological Review* 61:951–72.

Bobo, L., M. Oliver, J. Johnson, and A. Valenzuela, Jr., eds. 2000. *Prismatic Metropolis.* New York: Russell Sage.

Bogardus, E. 1925. "Measuring Social Distance." *Journal of Applied Sociology* 9:299–308.

———. 1950. "Stereotypes versus Sociotypes." *Sociology and Social Research* 34:286–91.

Brown, R. 1986. *Social Psychology: The Second Edition.* New York: Free Press.

Buruma, I., and A. Margalit. 2004. *Occidentalism: The West in the Eyes of Its Enemies.* New York: Penguin Press.

Callan, E. 2005. "The Ethics of Assimilation." *Ethics* 115:471–500.

Cattell, R., ed. 1966. *Handbook of Multivariate Experimental Psychology.* Chicago: Rand McNally.

Coenders, M., M. Lubbers, and P. Scheepers. 2004. "Majorities' Attitudes towards Minorities in European Union Member States: Results from the Standard Eurobarometers 1997–2000–2003." Report 2 for the European Monitoring Centre on Racism and Xenophobia. Ref. no. 2003/04/01.

Dovidio, J., P. Glick, and L. Rudman, eds. 2005. *On the Nature of Prejudice: Fifty Years after Allport.* Malden, MA: Blackwell.

Dubbelman, J., and J. Tanja, eds. 1987. *Vreemd gespuis.* Amsterdam: Ambo.

Duckitt, J. 2001. "Reducing Prejudice: An Historical and Multi-level Approach." In M. Augoustinous and K. Reynolds, ed., *Understanding Prejudice, Racism, and Social Conflict.* London: Sage.

Eagly, A., and A.B. Dickman. 2005. "What Is the Problem? Prejudice as an Attitude-in-Context." In J. Dovidio, P. Glick, and L. Rudman, eds., *On the Nature of Prejudice.* Malden, MA: Blackwell.

El fadl, K. A. 2002. *The Place of Tolerance in Islam.* Boston: Beacon Press.

Entzinger, H., and R. Beizeveld. 2003. *Benchmarking in Immigrant Integration.* Report for the European Commission, European Research Center on Migration and Ethnic Relations (ERCOMER).

Erikson, R., M. MacKuen, and J. Stimson. 2002. *The Macro Polity.* New York: Cambridge University Press.

Fetzer, J. 2000. *Public Attitudes toward Immigration in the United States, France and Germany.* New York: Cambridge University Press.

Gaertner, S., and J. Dovidio. 2000. *Reducing Intergroup Bias: The Common Ingroup Model.* Philadelphia: Taylor and Francis.

Gijsbers, M. 2005. "Opvattingen onder autochtonen en allochtonen over de multi-etnische samenleving" (Beliefs among indigenous Dutch and migrant groups about the multiethnic society). In Jaarrapport Integratie SCP. Den Haag: Sociaal Cultureel Planbureau. 189–205.

Golens, M., P. Sniderman, and J. Kuklinski. 1998. "Affirmative Action and the Politics of Realignment." *British Journal of Political Science* 28:159–83.

Hagendoorn, L. 1993. "Ethnic Categorization and Out-group Exclusion: The Role of Cultural Values and Social Stereotypes in the Construction of Ethnic Hierarchies." *Ethnic and Racial Studies* 16:26–51.

———. 1995. "Inter-group Biases in Multiple Group Systems: The Perception of Ethnic Hierarchies." *European Review of Social Psychology* 6:199–228.

Hagendoorn, L., and J. Hraba. 1989. "Foreign, Different, Deviant, Seclusive and Working Class: Anchors to an Ethnic Hierarchy in Holland." *Ethnic and Racial Studies* 12:441–68.

Hagendoorn, L., and G. Kleinpenning. 1991. "The Contribution of Domain-Specific Stereotypes to Ethnic Social Distance." *British Journal of Social Psychology* 30:63–78.

Hagendoorn, L., and P. Sniderman. 2001. "Experimenting with a National Sample: A Dutch Survey of Prejudice." *Patterns of Prejudice* 35.19–31.

———. 2004. "Het conformisme effect: Sociale beinvloeding van de houding ten opzichte van etnische minderheden." *Mens en Maatschappij* 79:101–23.

Hagendoorn, L., J. Veenman, and W. Vollebergh, eds. 2003a. *Integrating Immigrants in the Netherlands: Cultural versus Socio-economic Integration* Aldershot: Ashgate.

———. 2003b. "Cultural Orientation and Socio-Economic Integration of Immigrants in the Netherlands." In L. Hagendoorn, J. Veenman, and W. Vollebergh, eds., *Integrating Immigrants in the Netherlands: Cultural versus Socio-economic Integration*. Aldershot: Ashgate. 1–15.

Hambleton, R., H. Swaminathan, and H. Rogers. 1991. *Fundamentals of Item Response Theory*. Newburry Park: Sage.

Hardin, R. 1995. *One for All: The Logic of Group Conflict*. Princeton: Princeton University Press.

Henard, D. 2004. "Item Response Theory." In L. G. Grimm and P. R. Yarnold, eds., *Reading and Understanding More Multivariate Statistics*. Washington, DC: American Psychological Association.

Hollis, M. 2002. "Is Universalism Ethnocentric?" In C. Joppke and S. Lukes, eds., *Multicultural Questions*. Oxford: Oxford University Press. 27–43.

Horton, J., ed. 1993. *Liberalism, Multiculturalism, and Toleration*. London: Macmillan.

Huddy, L. 2001. "From Social to Political Identity: A Critical Examination of Social Identity Theory." *Political Psychology* 22:127–56.

———. 2002. "The Role of Context within Social Identity Theory: A Response to Oakes." *Political Psychology* 23:825–38.

Iyengar, S., and D. Kinder. 1987. *News That Matters*. Chicago: University of Chicago Press.

Jaarrapport Integratie SCP. 2005. Den Haag: Sociaal Cultureel Planbureau.

Jackman, M. 2005. "Rejection or Inclusion of Outgroups?" In J. Dovidio, P. Glick, and L. Rudman, eds., *On the Nature of Prejudice*. Malden, MA: Blackwell.

Joppke, C. 2005. *Selecting by Origin*. Cambridge, MA: Harvard University Press.

Kahneman, D., and A. Tversky. 1984. "Choices, Values, and Frames." *American Psychologist* 39:341–50.

Kaiser, H.F. 1960. "The Application of Electronic Computers to Factor Analysis." *Educational and Psychological Measurement* 20:141–51.

Kitschelt, H. 1997. *The Radical Right in Western Europe: A Comparative Analysis*. Ann Arbor: University of Michigan Press.

Koopmans, R. 2005. "*Tradeoffs between Equality and Difference—The Failure of Dutch Multiculturalism in Cross-National Perspective*." Paper for the Immigrant Political Incorporating conference, Radcliffe Institute for Advanced Study, Harvard University, April 22–23.

Koopmans, R., P. Stathn, M. Giugni, and F. Passy. 2005. *Contested Citizenship: Immigration and Cultural Diversity in Europe*. Minneapolis, MN: University of Minnesota Press.

Kuklinski J. 1997. "Public Opinion and Affirmative Action." *American Journal of Political Science* 41 (April): 402–19.

Kuklinski, J., and M. Cobb. 1998. "When White Southerners Converse about Race." In Jon Hurwitz and Mark Peffley," eds., *Perception and Prejudice*. New Haven: Yale University Press.

Kuklinski, J., M. Cobb, and M. Gilens. 1997. "Racial Attitudes and the 'New South.'" *Journal of Politics* 59:323–49.

Kuklinski, J., M. Gilens, and P. Sniderman. 1998. "Affirmative Action and the Politics of Realignment." *British Journal of Political Science*. 28:159–83.

Lijphart, A. 1977. *Democracy in Plural Societies: A Comparative Exploration*. New Haven: Yale University Press.

Lipset, S., and S. Rokkan. 1967. *Party Systems and Voter Alignments: Cross National Perspectives*. New York: Free Press.

Lucassen, L. 1987. "*Poepen, knoeten, mieren en moffen*." In J. Dubbelman and J. Tanja, eds., *Vreemd gespuis*. Amsterdam: Ambo. 29–37.

Luhtanen, R., and J. Crocker. 1992. "A Collective Self-Esteem Scale: Self-evaluation of One's Social Identity." *Personality and Social Psychology Bulletin* 18:302–18.

McCauley, C., and C. Stitt. 1978. "An Individual and Quantitative Measure of Stereotypes." *Journal of Personality and Social Psychology* 36:929–40.

McCauley, C., C. Stitt, and M. Segal. 1980. "Stereotyping: From Prejudice to Prediction." *Psychological Bulletin* 87:195–208.

Marcus, G., J. Sullivan, E. Theiss-Morse, and S. Wood. 1995. *With Malice toward
Some: How People Make Civil Liberties Judgments.* New York: Cambridge University Press.

Miller, D. 1999. *Principles of Social Justice.* Cambridge, MA: Harvard University
Press.

———. 2000. *Citizenship and National Identity.* Malden, MA: Blackwell.

Oakes, P. 2002. "Psychological Groups and Political Psychology: A Response to
Huddy's 'Critical Examination of Social Identity Theory.'" *Political Psychology*
23:809–24.

Oakes P., and A. Haslam. 2001. "Distortion v. Meaning: Categorization on Trial for
Inciting Group Hatred." In M. Augoustinos and K. Reynolds, eds., *Understanding Prejudice, Racism, and Social Conflict.* London: Sage, 179–94.

Okin, S. 1999. *Is Multiculturalism Bad for Women?* Princeton: Princeton University
Press.

Parekh, B. 2000. *Rethinking Multiculturalism: Cultural Diversity and Political Theory.* Cambridge, MA: Harvard University Press.

Penninx, R. 1988. *Minderheidsvorming en emancipatie: Balans van kennisverwerving
ten aanzien van immigranten en woonwagenbewoners 1967–1987.* Alphen aan den
Rijn: Samsom.

Phalet, K., and L. Hagendoorn. 2003. *Constructing and Mobilizing Ethno-religious
Identity and Otherness: Muslim Communities in a Multicultural City.* Utrecht: European Research Center on Migration and Ethnic Relations (ERCOMER).

Phalet, K., and A. Orkeny. 2001. "Ethnic Minorities and Inter-Ethnic Relations:
National Configurations and Cross-National Dimensions." In Karen Phalet and
Antal Orkeny, eds., *Ethnic Minorities and Inter-ethnic Relations in Context: A
Dutch Hungarian Comparison.* Research in Migration and Ethnic Relations Series.
Aldershot: Ashgate.

Phalet, K., and M. Swyngedouw. 2004. "A Cross-Cultural Analysis of Host and
Immigrant Acculturation and Value Orientations." In H. Vinken, J. Soeters, and
P. Ester., eds., *Comparing Cultures: Dimensions of Culture in a Comparative Per-
spective.* Leiden: Brill. 185–212.

Phalet, K., C. VanLotringen, and H. Entzinger. 2000. *Islam in de multiculturele
samenleving.* ERCOMER Report 2000(1) Utrecht: Utrecht University.

Philips, A. 1999. "The Politicisation of Difference: Does This Make for a More Intolerant Society?" In J. Horton and S. Mendus, eds., *Toleration, Identity and Difference.* New York: St. Martin's Press.

Quillian, L. 1995. "Prejudice as a Response to Perceived Group Threat." *American Sociological Review* 60:586–611.

———. 1996. "Group Threat and Regional Change in Attitudes towards African-Americans." *American Journal of Sociology* 102:816–60.

Reich, R. 2002. *Bridging Liberalism and Multiculturalism in American Education.* Chicago: University of Chicago Press.

Reicher, S. 2004. "The Context of Social Identity: Domination, Resistance, and Change." *Political Psychology* 25:921–46.

Robinson, W. 1996. "Postscript." In W. P. Robinson, ed., *Social Groups and Identities.* Oxford: Butterworth-Heineman.

Rogers, H., H. Swaminathan, and H. Rogers. 1991. *Fundamentals of Item Response Theory.* Newburry Park: Sage.

Scanlon, T. 2003. *The Difficulty of Tolerance: Essays in Political Philosophy.* New York: Cambridge University Press.

Schama, S. 1987. *The Embarrassment of Riches: On the Dutch Golden Age.* New York: Knopf.

Schoenfeld, G. 2004. *The Return of Anti-Semitism.* San Francisco: Encounter Books.

Sears, D., and C. Funk. 1990. "Self-Interest in Americans' Political Opinions." In J. Mansbridge, ed., *Beyond Self-interest.* Chicago: University of Chicago Press.

Sears, D., J. Sidanius, and L. Bobo, eds. 1999. *Racialized Politics: The Debate about Racism in America.* Chicago: University of Chicago Press.

Scheepers, P., M. Gijsbers, and M. Coenders. 2002. "Ethnic Exclusionism in European Countries: Public Opposition to Civil Rights for Legal Migrants as a Response to Perceived Ethnic Threat." *European Sociological Review* 18:17–34.

Sniderman, P., and E. G. Carmines. 1997. *Reaching beyond Race.* Cambridge, MA: Harvard University Press.

Sniderman, P., and T. Piazza. 1993. *The Scar of Race.* Cambridge, MA: Harvard University Press.

Sniderman, P., L. Hagendoorn, and M. Prior. 2003. "De moeizame acceptatie van moslims in Nederland." *Mens en Maatschappij* 78:199–217.

———. 2004. "Predispositional Factors and Situational Triggers: Exclusionary Reactions to Immigrant Minorities." *American Political Science Review* 98:35–50.

Sniderman, P., J. Fletcher, P. Russell, and P. Tetlock. 1996. The Clash of Rights: Liberty, Equality, and Legitimacy in Pluralist Democracies. New Haven: Yale University Press.

Sniderman, P., P. Peri, R. De Figuerido, and T. Piazza. 2000. *The Outsider: Prejudice and Politics in Italy.* Princeton: Princeton University Press.

Sniderman, P., D. Northrup, J. Fletcher, P. Russell, and P. Tetlock. 1993. "Psychological and Cultural Foundations of Prejudice: The Case of Anti-Semitism in Quebec." *Canadian Review of Sociology and Anthropology* 30:242–70.

Stokes, S. 2000. "Perverse Accountability: A Formal Model of Machine Politics with Evidence from Argentina." *American Political Science Review* 99:315–25.

Tajfel, H. 1978. *The Social Psychology of Minorities.* London: Minority Rights Group.

———. 1981. *Human Groups and Social Categories: Studies in Social Psychology.* New York: Cambridge University Press.

———. 1982. *Social Identity and Intergroup Relations,* New York: Cambridge University Press.

Tanja, J. 1987. "Brabantse monsieurs, Vlaamse ijveraars en Hollantsche bottigheid." In J. Dubbelman and J. Tanja, eds., *Vreemd gespuis.* Amsterdam: Ambo.

Taylor, C. 1994. "The Politics of Recognition." In A. Gutmann, ed., *Multiculturalism: Examining the Politics of Recognition.* Princeton: Princeton University Press.

Turner, J. 1996. "Henri Tajfel: An Introduction." In W. Robinson, ed., *Social Groups and Identities: Developing the Legacy of Henri Tajfel.* Oxford: Butterworth-Heinemann.

Van Amersfoort, J. 1974. *Immigratie en minderheidsvorming: Een analyse van de Nederlandse situatie 1945–1973.* Alphen aan den Rijn: Samsom.

Van den Berg-Eldering, L. 1982. *Marokkaanse gezinnen in Nederland.* Alphen aan den Rijn: Samsom.

Van der Brug, W. 2003. "How the LPF Fuelled Discontent: Empirical Tests of Explanations of LPF Support." *Acta Politica* 38:89–106.

Van der Hoek, J. 1994. *Socialisatie in Migrantengezinnen.* Leiden: Lidesco.

Van Holsteyn, J., G. Irwin, and J. den Ridder. 2003. "In the Eye of the Beholder: The Perception of the List Pim Fortuyn and the Parliamentary Elections of May 2002." *Acta Politica* 38:69–87.

Van Praag, P. 2003. "The Winners and Losers in a Turbulent Year." *Acta Politica* 38:5–22.

Verkuyten, M. 1997. *Redelijk racisme.* Amsterdam: Amsterdam University Press.

———. 2005a. *The Social Psychology of Ethnic Identity.* London: Psychology Press.

———. 2005b. "Ethnic Group Identification and Group Evaluations among Minority and Majority Groups: Testing the Multiculturalism Hypothesis." *Journal of Personality and Social Psychology* 88:121–38.

———. 2005c. "Immigration Discourses and Their Impact on Multiculturalism: A Discursive and Experimental Study." *British Journal of Social Psychology* 44:223–41.

Verkuyten, M., and A. Yildiz. 2006. "The Endorsement of Minority Rights: The

Role of Group Position, National Context, and Ideological Beliefs." *Political Psychology* 27:527–48.

Verkuyten, M., and K. Zaremba. 2006. "Inter-ethnic Relations in a Changing Political Context." *Social Psychology Quarterly* 68:375–86.

Vermeulen, H., and R. Penninx, eds. 2001. *Immigrant Integration: The Dutch Case.* Amsterdam: Het Spinhuis.

Visser, J., and A. Hemerijck. 1997. *A Dutch Miracle: Job Growth, Welfare Reform and Corporatism in the Netherlands.* Amsterdam: Amsterdam University Press.

Zolberg, A., and L. Woon. 1999. "Why Islam Is Like Spanish: Cultural Incorporation in Europe and the United States." *Politics and Society* 27:5–38.